D1525332

GLOBALVIEWPOINTS

Life After Death? Inheritance, Burial Practices, and Family Heirlooms

Other Books in the Global Viewpoints Series

GLOBALVIEWPOINTS

Life After Death? Inheritance, Burial Practices, and Family Heirlooms

Marcia Amidon Lusted, Book Editor

GREENHAVEN
PUBLISHING

Published in 2019 by Greenhaven Publishing, LLC
353 3rd Avenue, Suite 255, New York, NY 10010

Copyright © 2019 by Greenhaven Publishing, LLC

First Edition

Articles in Greenhaven Publishing anthologies are often edited for length to meet page
requirements. In addition, original titles of these works are changed to clearly present
the main thesis and to explicitly indicate the author's opinion. Every effort is made to
ensure that Greenhaven Publishing accurately reflects the original intent of the authors.
Every effort has been made to trace the owners of the copyrighted material.

Cover image: George Steinmetz/Corbis Documentary/Getty Images
Map: frees/Shutterstock.com

Library of Congress Cataloging-in-Publication Data

Names: Lusted, Marcia Amidon, editor.
Title: Life after death? : inheritance, burial practices, and family
  heirlooms / Marcia Amidon Lusted, Book Editor.
Other titles: Life after death? (Greenhaven Publishing)
Description: First edition. | New York : Greenhaven Publishing, 2019. |
  Series: Global viewpoints | Includes bibliographical references and index.
  | Audience: Grade 9–12.
Identifiers: LCCN 2018026016| ISBN 9781534504202 (library bound) | ISBN
  9781534504776 (pbk.)
Subjects: LCSH: Funeral rites and ceremonies—Juvenile literature. | Mourning
  customs—Juvenile literature.
Classification: LCC GT3150 .L54 2019 | DDC 393—dc23
LC record available at https://lccn.loc.gov/2018026016

Manufactured in the United States of America

Website: http://greenhavenpublishing.com

Contents

Chapter 3: Inheritance and the Legalities of Death

Chapter 4: The Legacies That Linger After Death

Foreword

"*The problems of all of humanity can
only be solved by all of humanity.*"
—*Swiss author Friedrich Dürrenmatt*

Global interdependence has become an undeniable reality.
Mass media and technology have increased worldwide
access to information and created a society of global citizens.
Understanding and navigating this global community is a challenge,
requiring a high degree of information literacy and a new level of
learning sophistication.

Building on the success of its flagship series, Opposing
Viewpoints, Greenhaven Publishing has created the Global
Viewpoints series to examine a broad range of current, often
controversial topics of worldwide importance from a variety of
international perspectives. Providing students and other readers
with the information they need to explore global connections
and think critically about worldwide implications, each Global
Viewpoints volume offers a panoramic view of a topic of
widespread significance.

Drugs, famine, immigration—a broad, international treatment
is essential to do justice to social, environmental, health, and
political issues such as these. Junior high, high school, and early
college students, as well as general readers, can all use Global
Viewpoints anthologies to discern the complexities relating to each
issue. Readers will be able to examine unique national perspectives
while, at the same time, appreciating the interconnectedness that
global priorities bring to all nations and cultures.

Material in each volume is selected from a diverse range of
sources, including journals, magazines, newspapers, nonfiction
books, speeches, government documents, pamphlets, organization

newsletters, and position papers. Global Viewpoints is truly global, with material drawn primarily from international sources available in English and secondarily from US sources with extensive international coverage.

Features of each volume in the Global Viewpoints series include:

- An annotated table of contents that provides a brief summary of each essay in the volume, including the name of the country or area covered in the essay.

- An introduction specific to the volume topic.

- A world map to help readers locate the countries or areas covered in the essays.

- For each viewpoint, an introduction that contains notes about the author and source of the viewpoint explains why material from the specific country is being presented, summarizes the main points of the viewpoint, and offers three guided reading questions to aid in understanding and comprehension.

- For further discussion questions that promote critical thinking by asking the reader to compare and contrast aspects of the viewpoints or draw conclusions about perspectives and arguments.

- A worldwide list of organizations to contact for readers seeking additional information.

- A periodical bibliography for each chapter and a bibliography of books on the volume topic to aid in further research.

- A comprehensive subject index to offer access to people, places, events, and subjects cited in the text.

Global Viewpoints is designed for a broad spectrum of readers who want to learn more about current events, history, political science, government, international relations, economics, environmental science, world cultures, and sociology—students doing research for class assignments or debates, teachers and faculty seeking to supplement course materials, and others wanting to understand current issues better. By presenting how people in various countries perceive the root causes, current consequences, and proposed solutions to worldwide challenges, Global Viewpoints volumes offer readers opportunities to enhance their global awareness and their knowledge of cultures worldwide.

Introduction

"The life of the dead is placed in the memory of the living."
-*Marcus Tullius Cicero*

Of all human experiences, death is the most unknown and often the most frightening. As long as humans have inhabited the earth, they have dealt with death in different ways, developing cultural rituals to help them process death and grieving as well as trying to formulate answers to the great, unanswerable question of what happens to the human spirit and soul after the physical body dies.

Society has developed different ways to handle the end of life, especially when someone becomes ill or is clearly approaching the end of their life. In the past, people often died at home, cared for by relatives, sometimes due to illnesses and injuries that would be curable today. Sometimes an ill person who knew that death was near would go out into the wilderness to die alone. Today people are more likely to die in a hospital setting, which sometimes means that families make difficult decisions about when to prolong life, what is appropriate care, what measures should be taken for comfort, and how to respect the wishes of the dying as to how they end their lives. Many people today can also choose to enter hospice care when they have a terminal illness such as cancer. They are able to return to their own homes and be cared for by friends and family until they die, which in its own way is a return to a home-based form of death from hundreds of years ago.

Many cultures have rituals that revolve around religious beliefs in an afterlife, such as heaven or hell. Some see death as loss and sadness, while others view it as the person's release from the difficulties and sorrows of life into a more peaceful afterlife.

Cultures and religions also differ in how they handle the remains of loved ones after they die. In some cultures, cremation is normal, as bodies are burned on pyres or in crematoriums. Other cultures believe in burial, whether in the earth itself or within a mausoleum or crypt. Some cultures believe that the physical remains should be left in the open air to decay naturally. Some people will be buried in a cemetery or other consecrated ground, with a headstone or monument to memorialize their life. Others choose not to have a lasting remembrance, opting instead to have their ashes scattered in a special location, or kept in a box or urn in a loved one's home, or even, in a few cases, sent into space. There are as many different death rituals as there as cultures in the world.

In a world as complex as today, death often creates difficulties as to how to divide the deceased person's money and possessions, called their estate. Some people will clearly designate not only where they want their estate to go and who will receive what, but also how the end of their life will be handled from a physical care point of view. Those who die unexpectedly or at an untimely age may leave no directives at all for care and the distribution of their estate. This can lead to both legal and emotional conflicts within families and other survivors, as to who will receive what. The question of what to do with heirlooms and the remains of a household can also cause anxiety and difficulties.

Finally, every culture has its own way of remembering the dead after they are gone. From Day of the Dead and Memorial Day, to keeping the ashes of loved ones in the house, there are many different ways for people to remember those who have gone before and honor their memories. Death is a difficult subject for most people to deal with, both because it means the loss of beloved family and friends, but also because it reminds them of their own mortality. Dealing with the issues surrounding death can help make it easier to cope with, both before, during, and after it occurs. The issues surrounding death and how it is addressed around the world are explored in *Global Viewpoints: Life After Death? Inheritance, Burial Practices, and Family Heirlooms.*

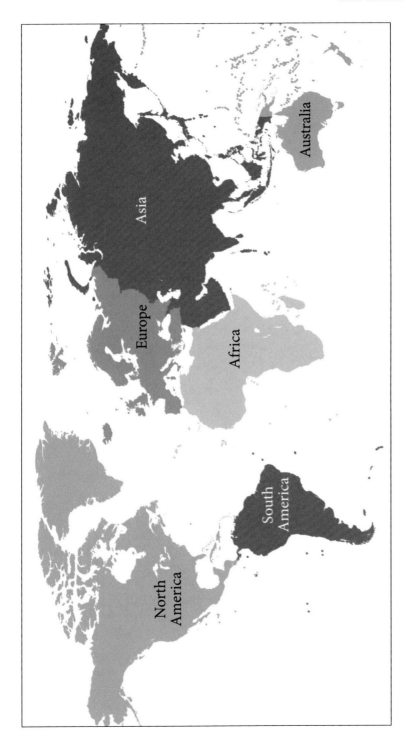

GLOBAL VIEWPOINTS

CHAPTER 1

Death and Dying Around the World

Dying in Comfort

Craig D. Blinderman and J. Andrew Billings

In the following viewpoint, Craig D. Blinderman and J. Andrew Billings argue that dying patients approaching the end of their lives have many specific physical and emotional needs, and that these needs should be addressed to provide the maximum level of comfort and calm possible. The authors provide caregivers and hospital personnel with specific issues to watch for, and how to alleviate them as much as possible. Blinderman is an Associate Professor of Medicine and the Director of the Adult Palliative Medicine Service at Columbia University Medical Center/New-York Presbyterian Hospital and Co-Director of the Center for Supportive Care and Clinical Ethics in the Department of Medicine. Billings was founding director of Massachusetts General Hospital's Palliative Care Service, cofounder of Harvard Medical School's Center for Palliative Care, and author of one of the first textbooks on hospice care.

As you read, consider the following questions:

1. What is meant by the term "comfort care"?
2. What kinds of goals should be set for the end of life?
3. What might be the definition of dyspnea, based on the information in the paragraph addressing it?

F or hospitalized patients whose death is imminent, palliative care can alleviate distressing symptoms that are common during the last few days or weeks of life. The essentials of such care that are presented in this review are intended to provide both generalists and specialists in fields other than palliative care with a practical, evidence-based approach to alleviating these symptoms in patients who are dying in a hospital. Communication skills that are essential to personalized care and goal setting are described briefly; the alleviation of the psychosocial and spiritual suffering that is often faced by terminally ill patients and their families is addressed only incidentally.

The term "comfort care" is used here to describe a set of the most basic palliative care interventions that provide immediate relief of symptoms in a patient who is very close to death. Typically, these measures are used to achieve comfort for the patient rapidly; diagnostic or therapeutic maneuvers that might be appropriate for palliation in earlier stages of the illness are usually not considered in this context. Many elements of this approach can be used to ease patients' distress in other phases of a life-threatening illness and in nonhospital settings, and they can also be applied to relieve symptoms in patients with less grave conditions.

The Need for Comfort-Care Skills in Hospital Practice

Although a growing proportion of deaths in the United States now occur at home or in nursing homes, hospitals remain a major site for end-of-life care; in 2010, 29% of deaths occurred in the hospital, and the average terminal admission lasted 7.9 days.[1]

Multiple distressing symptoms affect hospitalized patients who have advanced, life-threatening illnesses,[2,3] and some of these symptoms worsen as the patient approaches death.[4] Poorly controlled symptoms have been documented in patients with advanced cancer, congestive heart failure, chronic obstructive pulmonary disease (COPD), and many other life-threatening conditions.[5,6] The meticulous management of distressing symptoms is important in any phase of illness, but it becomes a primary focus near the end of life.[7]

Palliative care services can reduce the distress caused by symptoms and improve the quality of life of patients near the end of life.[8] However, the current scarcity of board-certified palliative care specialists—a workforce shortage that is projected to continue far into the future—means that the responsibility for ensuring excellent end-of-life care for dying patients will continue to fall primarily on generalists and on specialists in areas other than palliative care.[9,10] Thus, familiarity with basic comfort measures is an essential skill for all clinicians who are caring for patients whose death is imminent.[7,11]

Setting Goals at the End of Life: The Importance of Communication

The broad goals and methods of comfort care near the end of life should reflect the informed patient's wishes. The plan of care can then be aligned with the patient's wishes.[12] Such conversations about goals of care are essential when the withholding or withdrawing of life-sustaining interventions (e.g., dialysis or cardiopulmonary resuscitation) is being considered and as an aid in choosing appropriate diagnostic tests (e.g., positron-emission tomography–computed tomography or monitoring of vital signs). Discussions about setting goals at the end of life are associated with greater congruence between patients' wishes and the care that they receive during that time, and such discussions are correlated with the use of fewer aggressive, life-extending interventions (e.g., mechanical ventilation and resuscitation), as well as with end-of-life care that is consistent with the patient's preferences, fewer deaths in the intensive care unit, and earlier referral to a hospice.[17,18]

Understanding Comfort Care

Comfort care requires the meticulous palliation of troubling symptoms and offering of skilled psychosocial and spiritual support to the patient and the patient's family. However, the term is often used in a misleading or imprecise manner—for example, when such care is automatically considered equivalent to a do-not-resuscitate order and, perhaps even without discussion with the patient,[23] is extrapolated to mean the exclusion of a full range of palliative measures appropriate for a dying patient. Rather than simply writing orders for "comfort care" (or "intensive comfort measures," the term that we prefer), the medical team should review the entire plan of care and enter explicit orders to promote comfort and prevent unnecessary interventions.

Infrequently, a focus on comfort care may include the use of potentially life-sustaining measures, when these are consistent with a patient's goals (e.g., when the patient wants to be kept alive with mechanical ventilation until a loved one can visit from afar or when withdrawing a treatment conflicts with the patient's religious beliefs or cultural norms).[11] In addition, the use of invasive interventional procedures, such as thoracentesis for the treatment of symptomatic pleural effusions, can promote comfort.

Evidence-Based Management of Symptoms in Dying Patients

Here we offer basic guidance regarding the management of common symptoms that affect hospitalized patients whose death is imminent.[4] Because few high-quality studies address the management of symptoms in this population, we have often turned to investigations involving similar populations or to consensus statements on best practices for information. Our premise is that a brief, primarily pharmacologic, clinical guide should feature only a few essential, relatively inexpensive drugs that the clinician can become familiar with and learn to use confidently. Intravenous drug therapy is emphasized, since most hospitalized dying patients have an intravenous catheter, but suggestions for oral medications, which may be quite adequate in the hospital setting, are also included. If intravenous access is difficult to obtain, opioids and many other drugs can be administered conveniently by other routes, including through a subcutaneously placed butterfly needle that provides easy access for continuous or intermittent infusion.[24]

Pain

Pain is the symptom most feared by patients who have cancer and many other terminal conditions. Approximately 40% of hospitalized dying patients have moderate-to-severe pain in the final 3 days of life.[25] Assessment of this symptom should include regularly asking patients whether they have pain and, if so, to rate its severity. For example, "On a scale from 0 to 10, with 0 being no pain and 10 being the worst pain you can imagine, how much pain are you having now?"[26] Nonverbal indicators of discomfort (e.g., a patient's grimacing, moaning, or repeatedly rubbing a body part) can help the physician assess the severity of pain when patients are unable to provide a verbal response (e.g., in cases of advanced dementia).

Patients with mild pain (scores of 1 to 3 on a 10-point verbal reporting scale) should initially be treated with acetaminophen or a nonsteroidal anti-inflammatory drug (NSAID). If treatment with these agents fails to control pain, a low dose of an opioid can be added. If a patient who has been receiving oral opioids can no longer swallow, an equianalgesic intravenous regimen of the same opioid or, in the case of opioids that do not have an intravenous formulation, another agent should be substituted.

Opioids are first-line agents for the treatment of moderate-to-severe pain (pain score, 4 to 10 on a 10-point verbal reporting scale).[31] Morphine sulfate is commonly used; hydromorphone is an alternative. Oxycodone is a valuable oral agent, but there is no intravenous preparation. Various long-acting formulations, such as transdermal fentanyl patches, are appropriate for patients receiving stable opioid doses. Intravenous fentanyl has a number of advantages, primarily in critical care and perioperative settings. Methadone should be used only by clinicians who are familiar with its unique pharmacologic properties.

The initial management of moderate-to-severe pain should consist of frequent bolus doses of an opioid with rapid adjustment until a satisfactory degree of analgesia is achieved. When the patient is comfortable, the physician should prescribe a regular (basal) dose—which is typically administered as a continuous infusion—to prevent further pain, as well as intermittent bolus doses as needed for episodic worsening of pain ("breakthrough doses").

Constipation is a frequent side effect of opioid therapy and should be anticipated and treated prophylactically. Other common side effects of opioid therapy include sedation, confusion, nausea, pruritus, myoclonus, and urinary retention.[32] Inappropriate escalation of the opioid dose may result in unnecessary sedation and agitation at the end of life.[33] When opioid doses are adjusted appropriately, respiratory depression that is serious enough to affect survival is encountered only in rare cases.[34] Patients with renal failure, including those undergoing dialysis, are susceptible to neurotoxic effects of opioids, and special expertise is therefore needed for management of their care;[35] dose adjustments may also be required for patients who have liver failure. Rotation to another opioid should be considered when dose-limiting side effects, toxic effects, or incomplete analgesia occurs.[36]

Neuropathic pain should be distinguished from somatic or visceral pain, since opioids alone may not provide adequate analgesia for patients with neuropathic pain.[37] For patients with only a few days to live, adjuvant analgesics used for neuropathic pain may not have time to take effect; however, glucocorticoids may be of benefit in treating acute neuropathic pain.[38] The combination of morphine with gabapentin produces analgesia that is more effective than that provided by either agent alone.[39] Other agents (such as transdermal lidocaine, antidepressants, and anticonvulsants) may be considered when longer survival is anticipated.

Dyspnea
Dyspnea can be a debilitating symptom and may lead to substantial anxiety in the patient about the possibility of suffocating. A search for the underlying cause, especially when the degree of dyspnea changes rapidly, may occasionally be appropriate. However,

such investigations should not be allowed to delay the treatment of symptoms.

Opioids, given either orally or intravenously, are the treatment of choice for dyspnea and have been studied thoroughly in patients with COPD[40,41] and patients with cancer;[42] they have been found to be effective in alleviating dyspnea and, when used carefully, not to have serious side effects, such as respiratory depression.[43] Treating dyspnea with opioids is similar to managing moderate-to-severe pain, although lower opioid doses are typically adequate and safe for dyspnea.[41] For acute or severe dyspnea, intravenous morphine boluses should be used initially; after comfort is achieved, a continuous infusion may be started. When the patient is experiencing anxiety, as regularly occurs in association with breathlessness, benzodiazepines can be added, although there is no evidence that they have benefit in the treatment of the dyspnea itself.[45] Patients are regularly given supplemental oxygen for dyspnea, but systematic reviews have found no benefit for patients with cancer or heart failure who do not have hypoxemia;[46] however, oxygen may provide some relief for patients with COPD who do not have hypoxemia.[47]

Psychosocial support, relaxation, and breathing training can decrease breathlessness and distress.[48] Facial cooling with a fan reduces breathlessness.[49] In addition, patients may report benefiting from open windows, a reduction in ambient room temperature, breathing humidified air, and elevation of the head of the bed.[50]

When the withholding or withdrawal of mechanical ventilation is being considered for a patient with progressive dyspnea and this measure would be expected to lead quickly to death, patients and their families need to be reassured that the patient will not experience a sense of suffocation. Prophylactic intravenous bolus doses of both an opioid and a benzodiazepine should be given just before the ventilator is withdrawn, followed by further doses as needed.[51]

The presence of tachypnea or irregular breathing in an otherwise unresponsive patient should not be confused with the subjective feeling of dyspnea. Such actively dying patients often have altered respiratory patterns (e.g., Cheyne–Stokes breathing, intermittent apnea, or hyperpnea). The patient's family should be reassured that these breathing patterns are not distressing to the patient. Indeed, the aggressive use of opioid infusions for aberrant breathing patterns at the end of life can lead to opioid-induced toxic effects.[52]

Cough

Cough occurs at the end of life in up to 70% of patients with cancer and has been reported in 60% to nearly 100% of dying patients with various nonmalignant diseases.[53] Opioids, which act centrally to suppress the cough center, have been shown to be effective antitussive agents[54] and may work well at low doses.[55] Studies have also shown that gabapentin is effective for chronic cough.[56]

Xerostomia

Dry mouth, or xerostomia, is a common issue among patients at the end of life. Its causes include medications (e.g., anticholinergic agents, opioids, and antihistamines), radiotherapy to the head and neck, and dehydration. Strategies to minimize dry mouth include the discontinuation of unnecessary treatment with drugs that may contribute to the problem and the use of saliva stimulants, saliva substitutes, and other treatments. Parasympathomimetic medications (e.g., pilocarpine and cevimeline) are effective for improving xerostomia but are administered orally, so their use may not be practical for many dying patients.[57]

Excessive Oral and Pharyngeal Secretions

The inability to clear oral and tracheobronchial secretions is typically observed in the final days of life and can lead to gurgling sounds in the throat, sometimes referred to as a "death rattle." Although family members and staff are often distressed by these sounds, they are unlikely to be disturbing to the dying patient,[58] since they typically occur when the patient is unresponsive and lacks an effective cough reflex. The production of "grunting" sounds by the vocal cords is also common in dying patients.[59] Simply

Advance Directives

By thinking ahead and communicating treatment preferences early on, your loved one can prevent arguments and spare those close to him the anxiety of having to guess his wishes. Most important, he will have the opportunity to make very personal health care decisions for himself. These documents—called advanced directives—serve as a record of someone's medical preferences. To record his medical preferences, your loved one will need to complete written documents called advance directive forms. There are two types of advance directives, and it's important to have both:

1) A living will spells out what types of medical treatment a person wants at the end of life if he's unable to speak for himself. It tells medical professionals a person's wishes regarding specific decisions, such as whether to accept mechanical ventilation.

2) A health care power of attorney appoints someone to make health care decisions—and not just decisions regarding life-prolonging treatments—on one's behalf. The appointed health care agent (also called an attorney-in-fact or proxy) becomes the patient's spokesman and advocate on a range of medical treatments the patient sets out in the document.

Many states combine the two forms into one document, which can be used to record one's treatment preferences and name a health care advocate. The person your loved one appoints as his health care agent should know him well and be willing to carry out the directions your loved one has given to the agent regardless of personal feelings or influence from family and friends.

In addition to recording his wishes in advance directive documents, your loved one should discuss his values and health care goals with his agent. As the end draws near, some people find comfort in listening to music or having their favorite poems read. Others want family and friends to pray for them. Part of making his wishes known is sharing what's important to him. Your loved one also should keep copies of his advance directives in a safe and accessible place at home. He should specify their location in the letter of instruction that accompanies his will.

Planning for medical decisions without knowing what issues might arise isn't easy, but it's the responsible, compassionate thing to do for one's family. And when the time comes, knowing your loved one's wishes will give you peace of mind.

"Advance Directive: Creating a Living Will and Health Care Power of Attorney," American Association of Retired Persons (AARP).

repositioning the head may reduce these sounds and reassure loved ones that the patient is not in distress.

No convincing evidence beyond clinical reports supports the commonly recommended use of antimuscarinic agents (e.g., atropine and glycopyrrolate) in patients with noisy breathing due to terminal respiratory secretions.[60] A trial of glycopyrrolate can be considered, but we do not recommend its routine use, especially given the risk of such side effects as xerostomia, delirium, and sedation. Rather, clinicians should reassure and counsel family members and staff about the unlikelihood that the patient is experiencing discomfort from excessive secretions and about the lack of benefit and potential harm of treatment.

Nausea and Vomiting

Common causes of nausea and vomiting near the end of life include reactions to opioids and other medications, uremia, bowel obstruction, gastroparesis, ascites, and increased intracranial pressure. Some cases of nausea and vomiting can be treated according to their cause: glucocorticoids when symptoms are due to increased intracranial pressure,[61] metoclopramide in cases caused by gastroparesis,[62] muscarinic acetylcholine receptor antagonists (such as scopolamine) or antihistamines (such as promethazine) for symptoms of vestibular origin,[61] and perhaps octreotide and glucocorticoids for malignant bowel obstruction.[63]

Most episodes of nausea and vomiting near the end of life have multifactorial or uncertain causes.[64] The evidence supporting the efficacy of various antiemetics or of a single preferred agent in dying patients is limited. Haloperidol is recommended in much of the literature on palliative care, but metoclopramide is also favored.[61] Serotonin antagonists (e.g., ondansetron) are first-line agents in chemotherapy-related nausea and vomiting, and they may also be used alone or added to other dopamine-receptor antagonists, such as haloperidol, metoclopramide, and first-generation or second-generation antipsychotics (e.g., prochlorperazine and olanzapine).[61] Glucocorticoids are used in many situations, although a randomized, controlled trial comparing metoclopramide alone with metoclopramide plus glucocorticoids did not show a greater benefit in association with the latter regimen.[65] Benzodiazepines are used to prevent or treat anticipatory nausea and vomiting in patients receiving chemotherapy, but they may also have a more general role in treating nausea and vomiting when it is associated with anxiety.[61]

Constipation

Constipation is often multifactorial in terminal illness and typically results from dehydration, immobility, the effects of drugs, or the effects of a tumor on the bowel. Constipation is a predictable side effect of opioid use and needs to be managed prophylactically with a laxative regimen along with the opioid. Patients who can swallow oral medications are typically prescribed a stimulant laxative (such as senna) with a stool softener (such as docusate). No significant benefit has been found with the addition of docusate to senna alone.[66] Methylnaltrexone, an expensive drug that is indicated for opioid-induced constipation, is given subcutaneously and can be used to treat patients who are unable to swallow or whose conditions do not respond to the usual agents.[67,68]

Anorexia and Cachexia and the Role of Hydration and Nutrition

No drugs effectively treat anorexia and cachexia near the end of life, although glucocorticoid treatment can transiently improve appetite and energy.[50] The evidence from clinical studies does not support the use of artificial hydration or nutrition to improve symptoms of dehydration, quality of life, or survival in patients at the end of life.[69,70] Attempts to alleviate dehydration can result in fluid overload in these patients.

Even when this information is presented to patients and families, there may be considerable individual, cultural, or religious variation in their views of the acceptability of withholding fluids and nutrition. The physician should respect these personal values when making a recommendation, which must be tailored to the individual patient's situation; compromises are common (e.g., giving small amounts of parenteral water with dextrose despite the lack of evidence of benefit).

Fever

Dying patients may have troubling fevers in the final days or weeks of life. The cause is often unknown, but they may be due to infection, neoplasm, medication, or neurologic injury. Acetaminophen and NSAIDs are the first-line agents for the treatment of these fevers. Dexamethasone also has antipyretic properties and should be tried when treatment with the first-line agents fails. Antibiotics may have a role when a specific infection is being treated and when their use is consistent with the patient's goals (e.g., for alleviating a cough due to bronchitis), but they have not been shown to be generally effective in relieving fevers in the final week of life.[71]

Anxiety and Insomnia

A host of fears and concerns—about current or anticipated physical, psychological, social, and existential matters, including dying—are common among patients approaching death and may cause serious impairment of the quality of their remaining life or a frank anxiety disorder. Ensuring the patient's comfort will reduce his or her anxiety, but the primary treatment entails eliciting and addressing concerns and providing reassurance and support. Complementary therapies, such as relaxation exercises, may have a role, and mental health consultation should be considered. When symptoms of anxiety interfere with the patient's quality of life, pharmacotherapy may be considered, especially if some sedation is acceptable to the patient and the family. There is insufficient evidence for the recommendation of a pharmacologic treatment for anxiety at the end of life,[72] although the use of benzodiazepines is supported by consensus expert opinion.[73]

Sleep disorders are also common in patients near the end of life.[74] Physical discomfort is an important remediable cause.

Strategies for managing insomnia include nonpharmacologic interventions, such as ensuring that the patient's room is quiet and comfortable at night.[50] Little information is available to guide physicians in making a wise choice among hypnotic agents for use in the treatment of dying patients, but various shorter-acting benzodiazepines improve sleep[75] for terminally ill patients in whom anxiety is a principal cause of sleeplessness, among other groups of dying patients.[50] Nonbenzodiazepine hypnotic agents may also be useful.

Delirium

Confusional states are regularly encountered in patients as death approaches.[76] The cause is often multifactorial and may include organ failure, effects of medications, inadequately treated pain, disease of the central nervous system, and infection. The major features of these states include acute changes in the patient's level of consciousness (either hyperactive or hypoactive) or attention and disordered thinking, but delirium may also take a great variety of forms, such as restlessness or suspiciousness. Clinicians often overlook subtler forms of delirium, whereas family members unfortunately may misinterpret even moderately aberrant behavior by the patient as a reflection of normal cognitive processing (e.g., they may rationalize the patient's behavior as resulting from a lack of sleep).

There is little or no high-level evidence from meta-analyses or well-designed trials to guide the management of delirium in the terminal phase of life.[72,77] Antipsychotic agents are regularly used as the initial pharmacologic treatment. Haloperidol has long been the preferred initial treatment for both agitated, or hyperactive, delirium (characterized by agitation, restlessness, or emotional lability) and hypoactive delirium (characterized by flat affect, apathy, lethargy, or decreased responsiveness)[78] in patients receiving palliative care, but atypical antipsychotics (e.g., olanzapine and quetiapine) have recently been shown to be equally effective.[79] The familiarity with and versatility of haloperidol—it can be given both orally and parenterally—make it the preferred drug for initial use in patients with delirium.

There is insufficient evidence to recommend benzodiazepines for delirium,[80] except in cases of alcohol or sedative–hypnotic withdrawal.[81] Benzodiazepines can cause paradoxical reactions that worsen delirium, but they may be added cautiously if treatment with neuroleptic drugs fails to relieve agitation or if more sedation is desired.[79] Nonpharmacologic treatments for delirium include frequent reorientation to the environment and hospital routine, modification of factors that may precipitate delirium (such as sensory deprivation and pain),[82] and reductions in noise and other bothersome or stimulating environmental factors.

Palliative Sedation to Unconsciousness at the End of Life

Palliative sedation to the point of unconsciousness is a treatment of last resort when distressing symptoms cannot be controlled despite expert consultation.[83] It is widely recognized as an ethically appropriate approach in end-of-life care.[84] The goal is to relieve refractory suffering, not to hasten death, and it should not be confused with physician-assisted dying or voluntary euthanasia. The patient or a legal surrogate must be in agreement that such an approach is justified. Consultation with specialists in palliative care, ethics, psychiatry, or other areas should be considered before a decision to initiate palliative sedation is made.

Conclusions

Nearly a half century after the founding in London of St. Christopher's, the first modern hospice, in 1967, palliative care has been recognized throughout the world as an important medical specialty. Considerable advances have been made during that time in our knowledge of the management of symptoms in terminal illnesses—advances that deserve widespread incorporation into the clinical practice of both generalists and specialists. The information presented here should provide clinicians in fields other than palliative care with a framework for delivering basic comfort care to hospitalized patients who are near death.

Endnotes

1. Hall MJ, Levant S, DeFrances CJ. Trends in Inpatient Hospital Deaths: National Hospital Discharge Survey, 2000-2010. NCHS Data Brief2013:1-8.

2. McCarthy EP, Phillips RS, Zhong Z, Drews RE, Lynn J. Dying with Cancer: Patients' Function, Symptoms, and Care Preferences as Death Approaches. J Am Geriatr Soc 2000;48:Suppl:S110-S121.

3. Puntillo KA, Arai S, Cohen NH, et al. Symptoms Experienced by Intensive Care Unit Patients at High Risk of Dying. Crit Care Med 2010;38:2155-2160.

4. Hui D, Santos RD, Chisholm GB, Bruera E. Symptom Expression in the Last Seven Days of Life among Cancer Patients Admitted to Acute Palliative Care Units. J Pain Symptom Manage2014September19 (Epub ahead of print).

5. Levenson JW, McCarthy EP, Lynn J, Davis RB, Phillips RS. The Last Six Months of Life for Patients with Congestive Heart Failure. J Am Geriatr Soc 2000;48:Suppl:S101-S109.

6. Elkington H, White P, Addington-Hall J, Higgs R, Edmonds P. The Healthcare Needs of Chronic Obstructive Pulmonary Disease Patients in the Last Year of Life. Palliat Med 2005;19:485-491,

7. Institute of Medicine. Dying in America: Improving Quality and Honoring Individual Preferences Near the End of Life. Washington, DC: National Academies Press, 2014.

8. Higginson IJ, Evans CJ. What Is the Evidence that Palliative Care Teams Improve Outcomes for Cancer Patients and Their Families? Cancer J 2010;16:423-435.

9. Lupu D. Estimate of Current Hospice and Palliative Medicine Physician Workforce Shortage. J Pain Symptom Manage 2010;40:899-911.

10. Quill TE, Abernethy AP. Generalist plus specialist palliative care—creating a more sustainable model. N Engl J Med 2013;368:1173-1175.

11. Truog RD, Campbell ML, Curtis JR, et al. Recommendations for End-Of-Life Care in the Intensive Care Unit: A Consensus Statement By the American College [Corrected] of Critical Care Medicine. Crit Care Med 2008;36:953-963.

12. Bernacki RE, Block SD. Communication about Serious Illness Care Goals: A Review and Synthesis of Best Practices. JAMA Intern, Med 2014;174:1994-2003.

13. Back AL, Arnold RM, Baile WF, Tulsky JA, Fryer-Edwards K. Approaching Difficult Communication Tasks In Oncology. CA Cancer J Clin 2005;55:164-177.

14. Tulsky JA. Interventions to Enhance Communication among Patients, Providers, and Families. J Palliat Med 2005;8:Suppl 1:S95-S102.

15. Clayton JM, Hancock KM, Butow PN, et al. Clinical Practice Guidelines for Communicating Prognosis and End-of-Life Issues with Adults In the Advanced Stages of a Life-Limiting Illness, and Their Caregivers. Med J Aust 2007;186:Suppl 12:S77, S79, S83-108.

16. Blinderman CD, Krakauer EL, Solomon MZ. Time to Revise the Approach to Determining Cardiopulmonary Resuscitation Status. JAMA 2012;307:917-918.

17. Wright AA, Zhang B, Ray A, et al. Associations Between End-of-Life Discussions, Patient Mental Health, Medical Care Near Death, and Caregiver Bereavement Adjustment. JAMA 2008;300:1665-1673.

18. Mack JW, Weeks JC, Wright AA, Block SD, Prigerson HG. End-of-Life Discussions, Goal Attainment, and Distress at the End of Life: Predictors and Outcomes of Receipt of Care Consistent with Preferences. J Clin Oncol 2010;28:1203-1208.

19. Kutner JS, Blatchford PJ, Taylor DH Jr, et al. Safety and Benefit of Discontinuing Statin Therapy In the Setting of Advanced, Life-Limiting Illness: A Randomized Clinical Trial. JAMA Intern Med 2015;175:691-700.

20. Puntillo K, Ley SJ. Appropriately Timed Analgesics Control Pain Due to Chest Tube Removal. Am J Crit Care 2004;13:292-301.

21. Billings JA. Humane Terminal Extubation Reconsidered: The Role for Preemptive Analgesia and Sedation. Crit Care Med 2012;40:625-630.

22. Teno JM, Clarridge BR, Casey V, et al. Family Perspectives on End-Of-Life Care at the Last Place of Care. JAMA 2004;291:88-93.

23. Yuen JK, Reid MC, Fetters MD. Hospital Do-Not-Resuscitate Orders: Why They Have Failed and How to Fix Them. J Gen Intern Med 2011;26:791-797.

24. Parsons HA, Shukkoor A, Quan H, et al. Intermittent Subcutaneous Opioids for the Management of Cancer Pain. J Palliat Med 2008;11:1319-1324.

25. The SUPPORT Principal Investigators. A Controlled Trial to Improve Care for Seriously Ill Hospitalized Patients: The Study to Understand Prognoses and Preferences for Outcomes and Risks of Treatments (SUPPORT). JAMA 1995;274:1591-1598.

26. Jensen MP. The Validity and Reliability of Pain Measures in Adults with Cancer. J Pain 2003;4:2-21.

27. Swarm RA, Abernethy AP, Anghelescu DL, et al. Adult Cancer Pain. J Natl Compr Canc Netw 2013;11:992-1022.

28. Portenoy RK. Continuous Intravenous Infusion of Opioid Drugs. Med Clin North Am 1987;71:233-241.

29. Portenoy RK, Ahmed E. Principles of Opioid Use in Cancer Pain. J Clin Oncol 2014;32:1662-1670.

30. Breitbart W, Chandler S, Eagel B, et al. An Alternative Algorithm for Dosing Transdermal Fentanyl for Cancer-Related Pain. Oncology (Williston Park) 2000;14:695-705.

31. Caraceni A, Hanks G, Kaasa S, et al. Use of Opioid Analgesics in the Treatment of Cancer Pain: Evidence-Based Recommendations from the EAPC. Lancet Oncol 2012;13:e58-e68.

32. McNicol E, Horowicz-Mehler N, Fisk RA, et al. Management of Opioid Side Effects in Cancer-Related and Chronic Noncancer Pain: A Systematic Review. J Pain 2003;4:231-256.

33. White C, McCann MA, Jackson N. First Do No Harm . . . Terminal Restlessness or Drug-Induced Delirium. J Palliat Med 2007;10:345-351.

34. Morita T, Tsunoda J, Inoue S, Chihara S. Effects of High Dose Opioids and Sedatives On Survival in Terminally Ill Cancer Patients. J Pain Symptom Manage 2001;21:282-289.

35. Dean M. Opioids in Renal Failure and Dialysis Patients. J Pain Symptom Manage 2004;28:497-504.

36. Quigley C. Opioid Switching to Improve Pain Relief and Drug Tolerability. Cochrane Database Syst Rev2004:CD004847-CD004847.

37. McNicol ED, Midbari A, Eisenberg E. Opioids for Neuropathic Pain. Cochrane Database Syst Rev 2013;8:CD006146-CD006146.

38. Haywood A, Good P, Khan S, et al. Corticosteroids for the Management of Cancer-Related Pain in Adults. Cochrane Database Syst Rev 2015;4:CD010756-CD010756.

39. Gilron I, Bailey JM, Tu D, Holden RR, Weaver DF, Houlden RL. Morphine, Gabapentin, or Their Combination for Neuropathic Pain. N Engl J Med 2005;352:1324-1334.

40. Marciniuk DD, Goodridge D, Hernandez P, et al. Managing Dyspnea in Patients with Advanced Chronic Obstructive Pulmonary Disease: A Canadian Thoracic Society Clinical Practice Guideline. Can Respir J 2011;18:69-78.
41. Ekström MP, Bornefalk-Hermansson A, Abernethy AP, Currow DC. Safety of Benzodiazepines and Opioids in Very Severe Respiratory Disease: National Prospective Study. BMJ 2014;348:g445-g445.
42. Ben-Aharon I, Gafter-Gvili A, Paul M, Leibovici L, Stemmer SM. Interventions for Alleviating Cancer-Related Dyspnea: A Systematic Review. J Clin Oncol 2008;26:2396-2404.
43. Mahler DA, O'Donnell DE. Recent Advances in Dyspnea. Chest 2015;147:232-241.
44. Currow DC, Quinn S, Agar M, et al. Double-Blind, Placebo-Controlled, Randomized Trial of Octreotide in Malignant Bowel Obstruction. J Pain Symptom Manage 2015;49:814-821.
45. Simon ST, Higginson IJ, Booth S, Harding R, Bausewein C. Benzodiazepines for the Relief of Breathlessness in Advanced Malignant and Non-Malignant Diseases in Adults. Cochrane Database Syst Rev2010:CD007354-CD007354.
46. Cranston JM, Crockett A, Currow D. Oxygen Therapy for Dyspnoea in Adults. Cochrane Database Syst Rev2008:CD004769-CD004769.
47. Uronis H, McCrory DC, Samsa G, Currow D, Abernethy A. Symptomatic Oxygen for Non-Hypoxaemic Chronic Obstructive Pulmonary Disease. Cochrane Database Syst Rev2011:CD006429-CD006429.
48. Zhao I, Yates P. Non-Pharmacological Interventions for Breathlessness Management in Patients with Lung Cancer: A Systematic Review. Palliat Med 2008;22:693-701.
49. Galbraith S, Fagan P, Perkins P, Lynch A, Booth S. Does the Use of a Handheld Fan Improve Chronic Dyspnea? A Randomized, Controlled, Crossover Trial. J Pain Symptom Manage 2010;39:831-838.
50. Dy SM, Apostol CC. Evidence-Based Approaches to Other Symptoms in Advanced Cancer. Cancer J 2010;16:507-513.
51. Brody H, Campbell ML, Faber-Langendoen K, Ogle KS. Withdrawing Intensive Life-Sustaining Treatment—Recommendations for Compassionate Clinical Management. N Engl J Med 1997;336:652-657.
52. Blinderman CD. Opioids, Iatrogenic Harm and Disclosure of Medical Error. J Pain Symptom Manage 2010;39:309-313.
53. Bausewein C, Simon ST. Shortness of Breath and Cough in Patients in Palliative Care. Dtsch Arztebl Int 2013;110:563-571.
54. Chung KF. Drugs to Suppress Cough. Expert Opin Investig Drugs 2005;14:19-27.
55. Morice AH, Menon MS, Mulrennan SA, et al. Opiate Therapy in Chronic Cough. Am J Respir Crit Care Med 2007;175:312-315.
56. Ryan NM. A Review on the Efficacy and Safety of Gabapentin in the Treatment of Chronic Cough. Expert Opin Pharmacother 2015;16:135-145.
57. Villa A, Connell CL, Abati S. Diagnosis and Management of Xerostomia and Hyposalivation. Ther Clin Risk Manag 2015;11:45-51.
58. Lokker ME, van Zuylen L, van der Rijt CC, van der Heide A. Prevalence, Impact, and Treatment of Death Rattle: A Systematic Review. J Pain Symptom Manage 2014;47:105-122.
59. Hui D, Dos Santos R, Chisholm G, Bansal S, Souza Crovador C, Bruera E. Bedside Clinical Signs Associated with Impending Death in Patients with Advanced Cancer: Preliminary Findings of a Prospective, Longitudinal Cohort Study. Cancer 2015;121:960-967.

60. Wee B, Hillier R. Interventions for Noisy Breathing in Patients Near to Death. Cochrane Database Syst Rev2008:CD005177-CD005177.
61. Glare P, Miller J, Nikolova T, Tickoo R. Treating Nausea and Vomiting in Palliative Care: A Review. Clin Interv Aging 2011;6:243-259.
62. Acosta A, Camilleri M. Prokinetics in Gastroparesis. Gastroenterol Clin North Am 2015;44:97-111.
63. Longford E, Scott A, Fradsham S, et al. Malignant Bowel Obstruction—A Systematic Literature Review and Evaluation of Current Practice. BMJ Support Palliat Care 2015;5.
64. Davis MP, Hallerberg G. A Systematic Review of the Treatment of Nausea and/ or Vomiting in Cancer Unrelated to Chemotherapy or Radiation. J Pain Symptom Manage 2010;39:756-767.
65. Bruera E, Moyano JR, Sala R, et al. Dexamethasone in Addition to Metoclopramide for Chronic Nausea in Patients with Advanced Cancer: A Randomized Controlled Trial. J Pain Symptom Manage 2004;28:381-388.
66. Tarumi Y, Wilson MP, Szafran O, Spooner GR. Randomized, Double-Blind, Placebo-Controlled Trial of Oral Docusate in the Management of Constipation in Hospice Patients. J Pain Symptom Manage 2013;45:2-13.
67. Thomas J, Karver S, Cooney GA, et al. Methylnaltrexone for Opioid-Induced Constipation in Advanced Illness. N Engl J Med 2008;358:2332-2343.
68. Bull J, Wellman CV, Israel RJ, Barrett AC, Paterson C, Forbes WP. Fixed-Dose Subcutaneous Methylnaltrexone in Patients with Advanced Illness and Opioid-Induced Constipation: Results of a Randomized, Placebo-Controlled Study and Open-Label Extension. J Palliat Med 2015;18:593-600.
69. Bruera E, Hui D, Dalal S, et al. Parenteral Hydration in Patients with Advanced Cancer: A Multicenter, Double-Blind, Placebo-Controlled Randomized Trial. J Clin Oncol 2013;31:111-118.
70. Good P, Cavenagh J, Mather M, Ravenscroft P. Medically Assisted Nutrition for Palliative Care in Adult Patients. Cochrane Database Syst Rev2008:CD006274-CD006274.
71. Nakagawa S, Toya Y, Okamoto Y, et al. Can Anti-Infective Drugs Improve the Infection-Related Symptoms of Patients with Cancer During the Terminal Stages of Their Lives? J Palliat Med 2010;13:535-540.
72. Candy B, Jackson KC, Jones L, Leurent B, Tookman A, King M. Drug Therapy for Delirium in Terminally Ill Adult Patients. Cochrane Database Syst Rev 2012;11:CD004770-CD004770.
73. Lindqvist O, Lundquist G, Dickman A, et al. Four Essential Drugs Needed for Quality Care of the Dying: A Delphi-Study Based on International Expert Consensus Opinion. J Palliat Med 2013;16:38-43.
74. Savard J, Morin CM. Insomnia in the Context of Cancer: A Review of a Neglected Problem. J Clin Oncol 2001;19:895-908.
75. Holbrook AM, Crowther R, Lotter A, Cheng C, King D. Meta-Analysis of Benzodiazepine Use in the Treatment of Insomnia. CMAJ 2000;162:225-233.
76. Goy ER, Ganzini L. Prevalence and Natural History of Neuropsychiatric Syndromes in Veteran Hospice Patients. J Pain Symptom Manage 2011;41:394-401.

77. Bush SH, Leonard MM, Agar M, et al. End-Of-Life Delirium: Issues Regarding Recognition, Optimal Management, and the Role of Sedation in the Dying Phase. J Pain Symptom Manage 2014;48:215-230.

78. Breitbart W, Marotta R, Platt MM, et al. A Double-Blind Trial of Haloperidol, Chlorpromazine, and Lorazepam in the Treatment of Delirium in Hospitalized AIDS Patients. Am J Psychiatry 1996;153:231-237.

79. Grassi L, Caraceni A, Mitchell AJ, et al. Management of Delirium in Palliative Care: A Review. Curr Psychiatry Rep 2015;17:550-550.

80. Lonergan E, Luxenberg J, Areosa Sastre A. Benzodiazepines for Delirium. Cochrane Database Syst Rev 2009;4:CD006379-CD006379.

81. Schuckit MA. Recognition and Management of Withdrawal Delirium (Delirium Tremens). N Engl J Med 2014;371:2109-2113.

82. Inouye SK, Westendorp RG, Saczynski JS. Delirium in Elderly People. Lancet 2014;383:911-922.

83. Quill TE, Lo B, Brock DW, Meisel A. Last-Resort Options for Palliative Sedation. Ann Intern Med 2009;151:421-424.

84. Cherny NI, Radbruch L. European Association for Palliative Care (EAPC) Recommended Framework for the Use of Sedation in Palliative Care. Palliat Med 2009;23:581-593.

In the United States Culture Affects the End of Life

H. Russell Searight and Jennifer Gafford

The United States is a country with a large percentage of ethnic minorities. In the following viewpoint H. Russell Searight and Jennifer Gafford argue that when it comes to end of life care, caregivers and medical personnel need to be aware of the cultural differences among minorities. These differences may affect communication, decision making, and whether advance directives are created or followed as a patient nears the end. Being sensitive to cultural difference may make painful situations a little easier for minority individuals and families with strong cultural roots. Searight, PhD, MPH, is director of behavioral science at the Forest Park Hospital Family Medicine Residency Program in St. Louis, Missouri, and clinical associate professor of community and family medicine at Saint Louis University School of Medicine. Gafford, PhD, is faculty psychologist at the Forest Park Hospital Family Medicine Residency Program.

As you read, consider the following questions:

1. What are the three basic dimensions of end of life care that differ according to culture?
2. Why is it important for the US medical system to address different cultures?
3. What four dimensions are part of principlism?

Reprinted with permission "Cultural Diversity at the End of Life: Issues and Guidelines for Family Physicians," by H. Russell Searight and Jennifer Gafford, February 1, 2005, Vol 71, No 3, American Family Physician Copyright ©2005 American Academy of Family Physicians, All Rights Reserved.

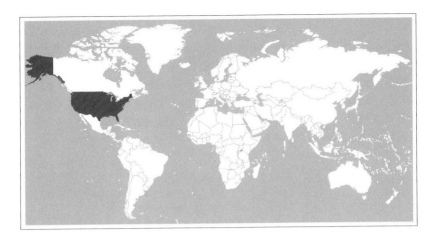

E thnic minorities currently compose approximately one third of the population of the United States. The US model of health care, which values autonomy in medical decision making, is not easily applied to members of some racial or ethnic groups. Cultural factors strongly influence patients' reactions to serious illness and decisions about end-of-life care. Research has identified three basic dimensions in end-of-life treatment that vary culturally: communication of "bad news"; locus of decision making; and attitudes toward advance directives and end-of-life care. In contrast to the emphasis on "truth telling" in the United States, it is not uncommon for health care professionals outside the United States to conceal serious diagnoses from patients, because disclosure of serious illness may be viewed as disrespectful, impolite, or even harmful to the patient. Similarly, with regard to decision making, the US emphasis on patient autonomy may contrast with preferences for more family-based, physician-based, or shared physician- and family-based decision making among some cultures. Finally, survey data suggest lower rates of advance directive completion among patients of specific ethnic backgrounds, which may reflect distrust of the US health care system, current health care disparities, cultural perspectives on death and suffering, and family dynamics. By paying attention to the patient's values, spirituality, and relationship dynamics, the family physician can elicit and follow cultural preferences.

Ethnic minorities compose an increasingly large proportion of the population of the United States. In the 2000 census, about 65 percent of the US population identified themselves as white, with the remaining percentage representing the following ethnic groups: black (13 percent); Hispanic (13 percent); Asian-Pacific Islander (4.5 percent); and American-Indian/Alaskan native (1.5 percent). About 2.5 percent of the population identify themselves as bi-ethnic, and this figure is likely to continue to grow.[1]

The challenge for family physicians in an increasingly diverse society is to learn how cultural factors influence patients' responses to medical issues such as healing and suffering, as well as the physician-patient relationship. The American Academy of Family Physicians (AAFP) has published cultural proficiency guidelines[2] and policy and advocacy statements about diversity in AAFP educational activities.[3] In addition, sensitivity to cultural diversity is integrated within the AAFP's policy statement on ethical principles for end-of-life care.[4] Specifically, principle 5 states: "Care at the end of life should recognize, assess, and address the psychological, social, spiritual/religious issues, and cultural taboos realizing that different cultures may require significantly different approaches."

Although cultural proficiency guidelines exist,[5] few resources are available to family physicians regarding ways to apply these guidelines to direct patient care. Many physicians are unfamiliar with common cultural variations regarding physician-patient communication, medical decision making, and attitudes about formal documents such as code status guidelines and advance directives. End-of-life discussions are particularly challenging because of their emotional and interpersonal intensity.

Physicians also are challenged by the tremendous diversity within specific ethnic minority groups.[6,7] In fact, research suggests that when compared with whites of European descent, ethnic minorities exhibit greater variability in their preferences.[8] Therefore, while certain styles of communication and decision making may be more common in some cultures, stereotyping should be avoided. Generalizations about specific cultures are not always applicable to specific patients.

Principlism, a well-established ethical framework for medical decisions in the United States and Western Europe, highlights cross-cultural differences that occur along four dimensions: autonomy, beneficence, nonmaleficence, and justice.[9,10] Although many patients in the United States value autonomy, other cultures emphasize beneficence. In the United States, legal documents such as advance directives and durable powers of attorney are strategies to prolong autonomy in situations in which patients can no longer represent themselves. Other cultures, however, de-emphasize autonomy, perceiving it as isolating rather than empowering. These non-Western cultures believe that communities and families, not individuals alone, are affected by life-threatening illnesses and the accompanying medical decisions.[11] Cultures valuing nonmaleficence (doing no harm) protect patients from the emotional and physical harm caused by directly addressing death and end-of-life care. Many Asian and Native American cultures value beneficence (physicians' obligation to promote patient welfare) by encouraging patient hope, even in the face of terminal illness.

Cultural influences in late-life care became particularly evident with the passing of the 1990 Federal Patient Self Determination Act (PSDA).[12] Case studies appeared that highlighted unforeseen dilemmas in the PSDA's implementation among some ethnic and cultural groups.[13,14] Subsequent research and case studies identified three basic dimensions in end-of-life treatment that may vary culturally: communication of "bad news," locus of decision making, and attitudes toward advance directives and end-of-life care.

Communicating Bad News

The consumer movement, legal requirements, an emphasis on patient informed consent, and reduced physician authority have contributed to health-related "truth telling" in the United States. Outside the United States, health care professionals often conceal serious diagnoses from patients. Physician strategies commonly employed to minimize direct disclosure include using terminology that obscures the seriousness of a condition or communicating diagnostic and treatment information only to the patient's family members. Many African and Japanese physicians, when discussing cancer with patients or family members, choose terms such as "growth," "mass," "blood disease," or "unclean tissue,"[15] rather than specifically describing a potentially terminal condition. In Hispanic, Chinese, and Pakistani communities, family members actively protect terminally ill patients from knowledge of their condition. In the United States, this protection may include deliberately not translating diagnosis and treatment information to patients,[16] a situation that is less likely to arise with appropriate use of a translator.[17,18]

There are four primary reasons for non-disclosure: (1) certain cultures specifically view discussion of serious illness and death as disrespectful or impolite;[5,19,20] (2) some cultures believe that open discussion of serious illness may provoke unnecessary depression or anxiety in the patient; (3) some cultures believe that direct disclosure may eliminate hope; and (4) some cultures believe that speaking aloud about a condition, even in a hypothetic sense, makes death or terminal illness real because of the power of the spoken word.

In many Asian cultures, it is perceived as unnecessarily cruel to directly inform a patient of a cancer diagnosis.[15,21] Even among people of European background, Bosnian-Americans and Italian-Americans perceive direct disclosure of illness as, at minimum, disrespectful, and more significantly, inhumane.[15,22] Recent immigrants to the United States described Bosnian physicians as "going around" the diagnosis and being indirect about serious illness in contrast to American physicians, whose directness they described as hurtful.[22]

Emotional reaction to news of serious illness is also considered directly harmful to health. It is thought that a patient who is already in pain should not have to grapple with feelings of depression as well.[21] This negative emotional impact on health also appears to be one of the primary reasons that Chinese patients are less likely to sign their own do-not-resuscitate (DNR) orders.[23] This concern, together with Asian values of reverence for aging family members,[7] may be especially pronounced in elderly patients who, because of their frailty, are perceived as more vulnerable to being upset by bad news. In addition, the special status of the elderly in Asian culture includes a value that they should not be burdened unnecessarily when they are ill.[11,15,24]

Direct disclosure of bad health news may eliminate patient hope. Bosnian respondents indicated that they expected physicians to maintain patients' optimism by not revealing terminal diagnoses.[22] Among other ethnic groups emphasizing this perspective of hope, there is the notion that factors outside of medical technology, such as a divine plan and personal coping skills, may be more important for survival than physician intervention.[5] Filipino patients may not want to discuss end-of-life care because these exchanges demonstrate a lack of respect for the belief that individual fate is determined by God.[24] If their hope is shattered, patients are no longer able to enjoy their daily lives and may feel they are "…among the dead while still alive."[11](p213)

Finally, Native American, Filipino, and Bosnian cultures emphasize that words should be carefully chosen because once spoken, they may become a reality. For example, a commonly held Navajo belief is that negative words and thoughts about health become self-fulfilling. Carrese and Rhodes[14] noted that Navajo informants place a particularly prominent value on thinking and speaking in a "positive way." About one half of their Navajo informants would not even discuss advance directives or anticipated therapeutic support status with patients because these verbal exchanges were considered potentially injurious. Similarly, the reluctance of Chinese patients and their families to discuss possible death is based on the belief that direct acknowledgement of mortality may be self-fulfilling.[23]

Locus of Decision Making

In the past 30 years, the US system of medical ethics has de-emphasized physician beneficence and increasingly emphasized patient autonomy. A patient's capacity for making independent decisions is questioned only if cognitive function or patient judgment appears to be impaired by medical or psychiatric illness. In contrast, many ethnic communities view it as appropriate to withhold potentially distressing information from cognitively intact, competent patients. Therefore, the North American cultural norm of individual decision making about medical care may have to be altered when physicians care for ethnically diverse patients. Alternate models of decision making include family-based, physician-based, and shared physician-family decision making.[5,19,25]

Cultures that place a higher value on beneficence and nonmaleficence relative to autonomy have a long tradition of family-centered health care decisions. In this collective decision process, relatives receive information about the patient's diagnosis and prognosis and make treatment choices, often without the patient's input. Compared with persons of black and European descent, Koreans and Mexican-Americans were more likely to consider family members, rather than the patient alone, as holding the decision-making power regarding life support.[9] With acculturation, Mexican-Americans were more likely to agree that patients should be directly informed of their conditions. However, acculturated Mexican-Americans continued to view decision making as a family-centered process.[5,8] Blacks may view an overly individualistic focus as disrespectful to their family heritage.[5,26,27]

Among Asian cultures, family-based medical decisions are a function of filial piety—an orientation toward the extended family as opposed to individual patient self-interest.[24] Illness is considered a family event rather than an individual occurrence.[11] Interests in Asian families are often bi-directional—there is an equivalent concern about the impact of the elderly person's death on the family.

Many societies attribute a high degree of authority, respect, and deference to physicians.[28-30] Patients and families defer end-of-life decisions to the physician, who is seen as an expert. Eastern European medicine has had a long tradition of physician-centered, paternalistic decision making. In Russian medicine, the physician rather than the patient or patient's family often unilaterally determines a patient's level of life support.[29] Recent Bosnian immigrants to the United States reported that they would prefer that physicians, because of their expert knowledge, make independent decisions to reduce the burden on patients and their families.[22]

In Asian, Indian, and Pakistani cultures, family members and physicians may share decisional duties. Family care of the terminally ill in Asian and Indian cultures is a shared responsibility for cognitively intact and incapacitated relatives. Physicians in Pakistan may be adopted into the family unit and addressed as parent, aunt, uncle, or sibling.[30] This family status provides the physician with a role sanctioning his or her involvement in intimate discussions.[30]

Advance Directives and End-of-Life Care

Survey data suggest that about 20 percent of the US population has advance directives.[31,32] Most investigators find significantly lower rates of advance directive completion among Asians, Hispanics, and blacks.[31,32] For example, about 40 percent of elderly white patients indicated that they had an advance directive, compared with only 16 percent of elderly blacks.[33] In one study,[8] none of the Korean respondents had advance directives, and relatively few of the Hispanics had completed these documents. The low rates of advance directive completion among non-whites may reflect distrust of the health care system, health care disparities, cultural perspectives on death and suffering, and family dynamics such as parent-child relationships.[5,19,25,34,35]

Among blacks, nonacceptance of advance directives appears to be part of a much broader pattern of values regarding quality of life, as well as a historical legacy of segregation. DNR orders may be viewed as a way of limiting expensive health care or as cutting costs by ceasing care prematurely.[11] Historically, this perspective may stem from a long history of distrust of the white-dominated health care system. The Tuskegee syphilis study,[36] in which infected black men were followed for 40 years but were not informed of the availability of penicillin treatment, is well known in the black community.

The reluctance of blacks to formally address end-of-life care also may stem from a history of health care discrimination. Although individual studies vary, the preponderance of evidence indicates that nonwhites, even after controlling for income, insurance status, and age, are less likely to receive a range of common medical interventions such as cardiac catheterization, immunizations, and analgesics for acute pain.[37,38] Although issues such as geographic patterns of medical care play some role in these disparities,[39] mistrust of the health care system is likely to be a factor in the lower rates of organ donation among blacks, as well as a reduced acceptance of hospice care.[40,41] Blacks with colon cancer were more likely than comparably ill white patients to want artificial nutrition, mechanical ventilation, and cardiopulmonary resuscitation.[41] Similarly, black patients overall are about one half as likely to accept DNR status and are more likely than whites to later change DNR orders to more aggressive levels of care.[42] These attitudes also carry over to black physicians, who are significantly more likely than their white colleagues to recommend aggressive treatment to patients with brain damage and known terminal illness.[43] Similarly, black physicians are less likely to accept physician-assisted suicide as an acceptable intervention.[43]

In addition to a historical legacy of unequal care, black patients also appear to view suffering somewhat differently than whites of European background. While whites may be concerned about dying patients undergoing needless suffering, black physicians and patients are more likely to think of suffering as spiritually meaningful, and life as always having some value.[11,44] Survival alone, even if it involves significant pain, may be an important demonstration of religious faith.[5]

Among Hispanics, the lack of acceptance of advance directives may stem from a view of collective family responsibility.[45] Hispanic patients may be reluctant to formally appoint a specific family member to be in charge because of concerns about isolating these persons or offending other relatives. Instead, a consensually oriented decision-making approach appears to be more acceptable in this population. Formalization of this process is seen as unnecessary and potentially harmful, because it may lead to increased and extended family conflict.[45]

Finally, among Asians, aggressive treatment for elderly family members is likely to be guided by filial piety. Asian adults feel a responsibility to reverently care for aging parents. This sense of obligation makes it difficult for relatives to request other than extraordinary measures.[20] Similarly, elderly Asian parents may experience a reciprocal obligation to continue living for the emotional well-being of their adult children.[20]

Guidelines for Cross-Cultural Communication

Physicians can actively develop rapport with ethnically diverse patients simply by demonstrating an interest in their cultural heritage. Attention to dimensions such as those listed,[6,7] should help physicians develop a more detailed understanding of important cultural issues. The power imbalance of physician-patient interaction may make it particularly difficult for ethnic minority patients to directly request culturally sensitive care. Through skillful use of patient-centered questions[5,19,25] and by including interpreters as necessary[17,18] physicians can develop a richer understanding of patients' health care preferences.

Patient preferences for nondisclosure of medical information and family-centered decision making may be disorienting initially to American-trained physicians. When treating patients from cultures with norms of nondisclosure, physicians might describe the dimensions of informed consent and offer to provide diagnostic and treatment information.[34,35] By offering autonomy to patients, cultural norms are respected while rights to independent decisions are simultaneously acknowledged.[46,47] A patient who refuses diagnostic information and prefers family-or physician-centered decision making has made a clear, voluntary choice. Physicians should also appreciate that, in certain cultures, while communication about serious illness and death may not be overt, information may be conveyed with subtlety. Facial expressions, voice tone, and other nonverbal cues may convey the seriousness of a patient's status without the necessity for explicit statements. In addition, stories about "good" deaths of family and community members may be shared with seriously ill patients.[14]

The physician's partnership with his or her patients and their families provides unique insight into their values, spirituality, and relationship dynamics, and may be especially helpful at the end of life. By eliciting and following cultural preferences regarding disclosure, advance planning, and decisional processes that relate to seriously ill patients, family physicians can provide culturally sensitive end-of-life care.

Endnotes

1. United States Census Bureau. US Census, 2000. Washington, D.C.: 2001.
2. American Academy of Family Physicians. Positions and Policies: Cultural Proficiency Guidelines (2001, 2003). Accessed online December 16, 2004, at: https://www.aafp.org/x6701.xml.
3. American Academy of Family Physicians. Positions and Policies: Diversity-Assuring Sensitivity to Diversity in AAFP Education (2000). Accessed online December 16, 2004, at: https://www.aafp.org/x6711.xml.
4. American Academy of Family Physicians. Position and Policies: Ethics, Core Principles for End-of-Life Care, Principle 5 (2000, 2002). Accessed online December 16, 2004, at: https://www.aafp.org/x6791.xml.
5. Kagawa-Singer M, Blackhall LJ. Negotiating Cross-Cultural Issues at the End of Life: "You Got to Go Where He Lives." JAMA. 2001;286:2993-3001.
6. McGoldrick M, Giordano J, Pearce JK, eds. Ethnicity and Family Therapy. 2d ed. New York: Guilford, 1996.
7. Searight HR. Family-of-Origin Therapy and Diversity. Washington, D.C.: Taylor & Francis, 1997.
8. Blackhall LJ, Murphy ST, Frank G, Michel V, Azen S. Ethnicity and Attitudes Toward Patient Autonomy. JAMA. 1995;274:820-5.
9. Beauchamp TL, Childress JF. Principles of Biomedical Ethics. 4th ed. New York: Oxford University Press, 1994.
10. Sugarman J, ed. 20 Common Problems: Ethics in Primary Care. New York: McGraw-Hill, 2000.
11. Candib LM. Truth Telling and Advance Planning at the End of Life: Problems with Autonomy in a Multicultural World. Fam Syst Health. 2002;20:213-28.

12. Federal Patient Self-Determination Act 19090, 42 U.S.C. 1395 cc(a).
13. Braun KL, Nichols R. Cultural Issues in Death and Dying. Hawaii Med J. 1996;55:260-64.
14. Carrese JA, Rhodes LA. Western Bioethics on the Navajo Reservation. Benefit or Harm? JAMA. 1995;274:826-9.
15. Holland JL, Geary N, Marchini A, Tross S. An International Survey of Physician Attitudes and Practice in Regard to Revealing the Diagnosis of Cancer. Cancer Invest. 1987;5:151-4.
16. Kaufert JM, Putsch RW. Communication through Interpreters in Healthcare: Ethical Dilemmas Arising from Differences in Class, Culture, Language, and Power. J Clin Ethics. 1997;8:71-87.
17. Herndon E, Joyce L. Getting the Most from Language Interpreters. Fam Pract Manag. 2004;11:37-40.
18. Flores G, Abreu M, Schwartz I, Hill M. The Importance of Language and Culture in Pediatric Care: Case Studies from the Latino Community. J Pediatr. 2000;137:842-8.
19. Hern HE Jr, Koenig BA, Moore LJ, Marshall PA. The Difference That Culture Can Make in End-of-Life Decision-Making. Camb Q Healthc Ethics. 1998;7:27-40.
20. Frank G, Blackhall LJ, Michel V, Murphy ST, Azen SP, Park K. A discourse of Relationships in Bioethics: Patient Autonomy and End-of-Life Decision Making among Elderly Korean Americans. Med Anthropol Q. 1998;12:403-23.
21. Matsumura S, Bito S, Liu H, Kahn K, Fukuhara S, Kagawa-Singer M, et al. Acculturation of Attitudes Toward End-of-Life Care: A Cross-Cultural Survey of Japanese Americans and Japanese. J Gen Intern Med. 2002;17:531-9.
22. Searight HR, Gafford J. "It's Like Playing with Your Destiny": Bosnian Immigrants' Views of Advance Directives and End-of-Life Decision-Making. J Immigr Health. [In press]
23. Liu JM, Lin WC, Chen YM, Wu HW, Yao NS, Chen LT, et al. The Status of the Do-Not-Resuscitate Order in Chinese Clinical Trial Patients in a Cancer Centre. J Med Ethics. 1999;25:309-14.
24. Yeo G, Hikuyeda N. Cultural Issues in End-of-Life Decision Making among Asians and Pacific Islanders in the United States. In: Braun K, Pietsch JH, Blanchette PL, eds. Cultural issues in end-of-life decision making. Thousand Oaks, Calif: Sage, 2000:101-25.
25. Ersek M, Kagawa-Singer M, Barnes D, Blackhall L, Koenig BA. Multicultural considerations in Use of Advance Directives. Oncol Nurs Forum. 1998;25:1683-90.
26. Waters CM. Understanding and Supporting African Americans' Perspectives of End-of-Life Care Planning and Decision Making. Qual Health Res. 2001;11:385-98.
27. Berger JT. Cultural Discrimination in Mechanisms for Health Decisions: A View from New York. J Clin Ethics. 1998;9:127-31.
28. Schlesinger M. A Loss of Faith: The Sources of Reduced Political Legitimacy for the American Medical Profession. Milbank Q. 2002;80:185-235.
29. Karakuzon M. Russia. In: Crippen D, Kilcullen JK, Kelly DF, eds. Three Patients: International Perspectives on Intensive Care at the End-of-Life. Boston: Kluwer, 2002:67-72.
30. Moazam F. Families, Patients, and Physicians in Medical Decisionmaking: A Pakistani Perspective. Hastings Cent Rep. 2000;30:28-37.
31. Pietch JH, Braun KL. Autonomy, Advance Directives, and the Patient Self-Determination Act. In: Braun K, Pietsch JH, Blanchette PL, eds. Cultural issues in end-of-life decision making. Thousand Oaks, Calif: Sage, 2000:37-53.
32. Baker ME. Economic, Political and Ethnic Influences on End-of-Life Decision-Making: A Decade in Review. J Health Soc Policy. 2002;14:27-39.

33. Hopp FP, Duffy SA. Racial Variations in End-of-Life Care. J Am Geriatr Soc. 2000;48:658-63.

34. Murphy ST, Palmer JM, Azen S, Frank G, Michel V, Blackhall L. Ethnicity and Advance Care Directives. J Law Med Ethics. 1996;24:108-17.

35. Flores G, Law MB, Mayo SJ, Zuckerman B, Abreu M, Medina L, et al. Errors in Medical Interpretation and Their Potential Clinical Consequences in Pediatric Encounters. Pediatrics. 2003;111:6-14.

36. Caplan AL. Twenty Years After: The Legacy of the Tuskegee Syphilis Study. In: Teays W, Purdy LM, eds. Bioethics, Justice and Health Care. Belmont, Calif.: Wadsworth-Thomson Learning, 2001:231-5.

37. Smedley BD, Stith AY, Nelson AR, eds. Unequal Treatment: Confronting Racial and Ethnic Disparities in Health Care. Washington, DC: National Academies Press, 2003.

38. Steinbrook R. Disparities in Health Care—from Politics to Policy. N Engl J Med. 2004;350:1486-8.

39. Lavizzo-Mourey R, Knickman JR. Racial Disparities—the Need for Research and Action. N Engl J Med. 2003;349:1379-80.

40. Siminoff LA, Lawrence RH, Arnold RM. Comparison of Black and White Families' Experiences and Perceptions Regarding Organ Donation Requests. Crit Care Med. 2003;31:146-51.

41. McKinley ED, Garrett JM, Evans AT, Danis M. Differences in End-of-Life Decision Making among Black and White Ambulatory Cancer Patients. J Gen Intern Med. 1996;11:651-6.

42. Tulsky JA, Cassileth BR, Bennett CL. The Effect of Ethnicity on ICU Use and DNR Orders in Hospitalized AIDS Patients. J Clin Ethics. 1997;8:150-7.

43. Mebane EW, Oman RF, Kroonen LT, Goldstein MK. The Influence of Physician Race, Age, and Gender on Physician Attitudes Toward Advance Care Directives and Preferences For End-of-Life Decision-Making. J Am Geriatr Soc. 1999;47:579-91.

44. Orona LJ, Koenig BA, Davis AJ. Cultural Aspects of Nondisclosure. Camb Q Healthc Ethics. 1994;3:338-46.

45. Morrison RS, Zayas LH, Mulvihill M, Baskin SA, Meier DE. Barriers to Completion of Healthcare Proxy Forms: A Qualitative Analysis of Ethnic Differences. J Clin Ethics. 1998;9:118-26.

46. Moskop JC. Informed Consent in the Emergency Department. Emerg Med Clin North Am. 1999;17:327-40.

47. Freedman B. Offering truth. One Ethical Approach to the Uninformed Cancer Patient. Arch Intern Med. 1993;153:572-6.

Advanced Directives Are Paths to Improved Well Being

American Academy of Family Physicians

For many people, the end of life necessitates making decisions about care and when to cease heroic medical measures to prolong life. In the following viewpoint, the need for advance directives about end of life care and when a patient should be allowed to die is emphasized as something that every person needs to have in place, especially as they get older. The American Academy of Family Physicians is one of the largest medical organizations in the United States. Its mission is to improve the health of patients, families, and communities by serving the needs of members with professionalism and creativity.

As you read, consider the following questions:

1. When might a legal directive for health care be necessary?
2. What is the difference between a living will and a durable power of attorney?
3. What is a DNR order, and why is it important?

An advance directive is a legal document. It tells your doctor and family what kind of medical care you want to have if you can't tell them yourself. This could happen if you:

- are in a coma
- are seriously injured

- are terminally ill

- have severe dementia.

If you are admitted to the hospital, the hospital staff will probably talk to you about advance directives.

Path to Improved Well Being

A good advance directive describes the kind of treatment you would want, depending on how sick you are. It could describe what kind of care you want if you have an illness that you are unlikely to recover from. It could also describe the care you want if you are permanently unconscious. Advance directives usually tell your doctor that you don't want certain kinds of treatment. They can also say that you want a certain treatment no matter how ill you are.

Advance directives could include:

Living Will

A living will is one type of advance directive. It is a written, legal document. It describes the treatments you would want if you were terminally ill or permanently unconscious. These could be medical treatments or treatments that will help you live longer. A living will doesn't let you select someone to make decisions for you.

Durable Power of Attorney for Health Care

A durable power of attorney (DPA) for health care is another kind of advance directive. A DPA states whom you have chosen to make health care decisions for you. It becomes active any time you are unconscious or unable to make medical decisions (and may be called Medical Power of Attorney, or MPOA). A DPA is generally more useful than a living will. But a DPA may not be a good choice if you don't have another person you trust to make these decisions for you.

Laws about advance directives are different in each state. Living wills and DPAs are legal in most states. These advance directives may not be officially recognized by the law in your state. But they can still guide your loved ones and doctor if you are unable to make decisions about your medical care. Ask your doctor, lawyer, or state representative about the laws in your state.

Physician Orders for Life-Sustaining Treatment (POLST)

A POLST is for people who have been diagnosed with a serious illness. It is filled out by your doctor. It doesn't replace your other advance directives. Instead it stays with you to ensure you get the medical treatment you want.

Do Not Resuscitate Order

A do-not-resuscitate (DNR) order can also be part of an advance directive. Hospital staff try to help any patient whose heart has stopped or who has stopped breathing. They do this with cardiopulmonary resuscitation (CPR). A DNR is a request not to have CPR if your heart stops or if you stop breathing. You can use an advance directive form or tell your doctor that you don't want to be resuscitated. Your doctor will put the DNR order in your medical chart. Doctors and hospitals in all states accept DNR orders. They do not have to be part of a living will or other advance directive.

Other possible end-of-life issues that may be covered in an advance directive include:

- Ventilation—if, and for how long, you want a machine to take over your breathing.

- Tube feeding—if, and for how long, you want to be fed through a tube in your stomach or through an IV.

- Palliative care (comfort care)—keeps you comfortable and manages pain. This could include receiving pain medicine or dying at home.

- Organ donation—specifying if you want to donate your organs, tissues, or body for other patients or for research.

Should I Have an Advance Directive?

Creating an advance directive is a good idea. It makes your preferences about medical care known before you're faced with a serious injury or illness. This will spare your loved ones the stress of making decisions about your care while you are sick. Any person 18 years of age or older can prepare an advance directive.

People who are seriously or terminally ill are more likely to have an advance directive. For example, someone who has terminal cancer might write that they do not want to be put on a respirator if they stop breathing. This action can reduce their suffering. It can increase their peace of mind, and give them more control over their death.

Even if you are in good health, you might want to consider writing an advance directive. An accident or serious illness can happen suddenly. If you already have a signed advance directive, your wishes are more likely to be followed.

How Can I Write an Advance Directive?
You can write an advance directive in several ways:

- Use a form provided by your doctor.

- Write your wishes down by yourself.

- Call your health department or state department on aging to get a form.

- Call a lawyer.

- Use a computer software package for legal documents.

Advance directives and living wills do not have to be complicated documents. They can be short, simple statements about what you want done or not done. Remember, anything you write by yourself or with a computer software package should follow your state laws. You may also want your doctor or a lawyer to review what you have written. They can make sure your directives are understood exactly as you intended. When you are satisfied with your directives, have the orders notarized. Then give copies to your family and your doctor.

Things to Consider

Can I Change My Advance Directive?

You may change or cancel your advance directive at any time, as long as you are of sound mind to do so. This means you can think rationally and communicate your wishes clearly. Again, your changes must be made, signed, and notarized according to the laws in your state. Make sure that your doctor and family members are aware of the changes.

If you change your mind, you can also make your changes known while you are in the hospital. Tell your doctor and any family or friends present exactly what you want to happen. Usually, wishes that are made in person will be followed in place of the ones made earlier in writing. Be sure your instructions are clearly understood by everyone you have told.

Questions to Ask Your Doctor

- I'm not sick. Do I need an advance directive?
- What kinds of things should I include in my advance directive?
- How do I go about getting one?
- Do I have to pay a lawyer to draw one up?
- What happens if I change my mind on the kind of care I want to receive?

In India a Final Fast Tradition Embraces Death and Looks Ahead to Life

Christopher Key Chapple

In the following viewpoint Christopher Key Chapple examines the Jain tradition of a final fast for those at the end of their lives. The fasting tradition is a rite of sorts that ushers a person from one life to the next. Jains believe they are eternal souls that take the forms of plants and microorganisms, eventually working their way up to humans through good works. The author argues that this practice celebrates a life lived and looks ahead to the next place their soul will land. Chapple is the Navin and Pratima Doshi Professor of Indic and Comparative Theology at Loyola Marymount University.

As you read, consider the following questions:

1. What is Santhara?
2. What do Jains believe is the key to spiritual ascent?
3. According to the author, what important lesson can the Jain tradition of the rite of passing from the human body teach us?

On June 9, a law allowing patients with terminal illnesses to end their lives with help from a physician came into effect in

"Aid to Dying: What Jainism—One of India's Oldest Religions—Teaches Us," by Christopher Key Chapple, The Conversation, June 10, 2016. https://theconversation.com/aid-to-dying-what-jainism-one-of-indias-oldest-religions-teaches-us-60828 Licensed under CC BY-ND 4.0 International.

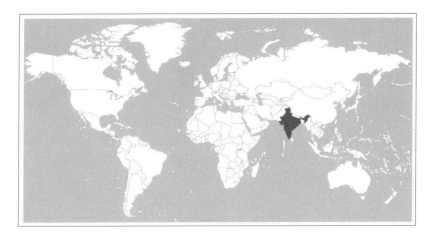

California, opening conversations about whether human life should be prolonged against the desire to die peacefully and with dignity.

A similar yet different conversation has been taking place in India for the past several years, but in reverse.

In one of India's religious traditions, Jainism, those at the end of life can choose to embrace a final fast transition from one body to another. However, a recent court case has challenged the constitutionality of this practice. As an expert in the religions of India and a frequent visitor, I have been following this issue with keen interest.

A Rite to Final Passage

While on a visit to a Jain university in Ladnun, Rajasthan in western India in 1989, I had an opportunity to observe the practice of "Sallekhana" or "Santhara," a somber rite through which one fasts to death.

A group of enthusiastic nuns rushed me in for a blessing being imparted to an octogenarian nun, Sadhvi Kesharji, who had taken this vow 28 days earlier. The nun had been diagnosed with a fatal kidney disease and been treated, but to no avail.

It was an auspicious moment. Her spiritual preceptor, Acharya Tulsi, praised her six decades as a nun and noted the lightness of her spirit and the strength of her resolve which guaranteed safe passage into her next incarnation.

She passed away 12 days later, in a prayerful state.

This is not the only such case. It is estimated that some 200 Jains, both lay and monastic, complete the final fast each year. Jains living elsewhere in the world observe the practice as well.

For example, two Jain women who were born in India but spent most of their adult lives in the United States chose to fast in the last days prior to death. Vijay Bhade, a Jain woman from West Virginia, entered a fast unto death in 1997. A more recent case was Bhagwati Gada, from Texas, who suffered from advanced stage cancer and decided to fast unto death in 2013, after going through multiple rounds of chemotherapy.

Who Are the Jains?

Jainism arose more than 2,800 years ago in northeast India. It teaches a doctrine proclaiming the existence of countless eternal souls who, due to their actions or karma, bind themselves to repeated lifetimes.

These souls could manifest as elemental beings in the earth or water or fire or air. They could evolve to become micro-organisms and plants or eventually take forms as worms, insects, birds, reptiles or mammals.

By committing acts of goodness, they might take human form and ascend to a place of everlasting freedom at the highest limits of the universe, from which they continue to observe forever the repeated rounds of existence experienced by the many souls below.

Jains do not believe in a creator God or an external controller. All experiences, good and bad, are due to one's own exertions. The key to spiritual ascent resides in the performance of five vows also shared by Yogis and Buddhists in India: nonviolence, truthfulness, not stealing, celibacy and nonpossession.

Jains believe the practice of these vows helps release fettering karmas that impede the energy, consciousness and bliss of the soul. Every ethical success lightens the soul of its karmic burden.

Pulling the Plug

Recently, I saw an illustration that accompanied an article about euthanasia. It showed the silhouette of a patient lying on a bed. There was an electrical outlet on the wall behind the bed and an unplugged connecting cord hanging down over the side of the bed. Except in very rare circumstances—for instance, if the treatment were withdrawn without the necessary consent or against the patient's wishes—withdrawal of life-support treatment is not euthanasia. Yet many people, including the artist who penned this illustration and many health-care professionals, mistakenly believe that it is.

In my experience, they are confused with respect to the ethical and legal differences between withdrawal of treatment that results in death and euthanasia, and why the former can be ethically and legally acceptable, provided certain conditions are fulfilled, and the latter cannot be. This is a central and important distinction in the euthanasia debate, which needs to be understood.

Failure to understand it leads, among other problems, to physicians responding affirmatively to surveys that ask them whether they or their colleagues have carried out euthanasia, when in fact they have not, and members of the public saying they agree with euthanasia, because they agree with people's rights to refuse medical treatment.

First, the primary intention is different in the two cases: In withdrawing life-support treatment the primary intention is to respect the patient's right to refuse treatment; in euthanasia it is to kill the patient. The former intention is ethically and legally acceptable; the latter is not.

Patients have a right to refuse treatment, even if that means they will die. They have a right not to be touched, including through medical treatment, without their consent—a right to inviolability. This right protects a person's physical integrity and can also function to protect physical and mental privacy. The right to inviolability is one aspect of every competent adult's right to autonomy and self-determination.

Pro-euthanasia advocates use recognition of this right to refuse treatment even when it results in death to argue that, likewise, patients should be allowed to exercise their right to autonomy and self-determination to choose death through lethal injection. They say that there is no morally or ethically significant difference between these situations, and there ought to be no legal difference.

"'Pulling the plug' isn't euthanasia," by Margaret Somerville, March 19, 2010, Consciencelaws.org.

Mohandas Gandhi, the well-known leader of India's independence, who grew up in the company of Jains, employed these vows personally and as a collective strategy of nonviolence to help India overcome the shackles of British colonization.

Freedom Yes, but Can There Be Coercion?

Up until recent years, the fast unto death process has been celebrated with newspaper announcements that laud the monks, nuns, laymen and laywomen who undergo this vow. But of late, questions are being raised whether it can result in coercion and cruelty.

In 2006, a young lawyer in Rajasthan, Nikhil Soni, challenged the constitutionality of this act, stating that it violates the anti-suicide laws that had been in put place by the British to stop the immolation of widows on their husband's funeral pyre. The practice of widow burning has endured, despite many efforts to abolish the practice.

The high court of Rajasthan ruled in favor of Soni in 2015, effectively making the practice of fasting to death punishable by law. However, some weeks later, the Supreme Court of India placed a stay on this ruling. The case is still awaiting its final verdict. Observant Jains claim this is an important part of their faith.

Entering the fast requires counsel and permission from one's spiritual advisor. And the process of rejection of food is gradual. First, one takes some yogurt, then only milk, then only juice, eventually moving from water to total rejection of any nutrition or hydration.

Physicians state that this is not death by starvation but by dehydration. The body automatically goes into a state of ketosis (when the body starts to break down stored fat for energy), often accompanied by a peaceful state.

Rights Versus Rites Approach

What can we learn from such spiritual practices?

Debates on end of life focus on the "rights" approach, thus appealing to the rational mind. Spiritual traditions on the other hand assert that it makes no sense to prolong suffering. They use a "rites" approach to the inevitable passing of the human body.

Jains believe that the soul has always been here, that the soul cannot be destroyed and that through the process of death, one transitions to a new body.

The Jain tradition shows how we can move without attachment into death rather than clinging to life. In their acceptance of the inevitable, they set an example that death is not an evil but an opportunity to reflect on a life well-lived and look forward to what lies ahead.

Having a Plan Can Ease the End-of-Life Journey

Sameera Karnik and Amar Kanekar

In the following viewpoint Sameera Karnik and Amar Kanekar discuss the end of life and the ethical issues that are involved in that process. In particular, they discuss how advancing medical technologies make it possible to prolong life even in extreme circumstances, and how this makes it vital for patients to have advance directives in place for how they want to end their lives. Karnik is in the Masters of Public Health program at American Public University. Dr. Kanekar is associate professor and graduate counselor at the School of Counseling, Human Performance and Rehabilitation at the University of Arkansas at Little Rock.

As you read, consider the following questions:

1. How does medical technology affect decision-making about the end of life?
2. Why is it important to respect the patient's own voice about the end of life?
3. What are the two types of advance directives? Why are both important to have?

All human-beings are mortals and hence death is an inevitable occurrence. Advancements in medical technology are changing the norms of natural death. These technologically advanced treatments have a capability to intervene at the time of death and prolong the lives of people. Medical technologies are facilitating to reshape the circumstances around natural death, by sustaining human lives. Even though medical treatments have advanced technologically they hold no promises for recovery, they can sustain life with or without meaningful existence or with secondary support (like feeding tubes, ventilators, etc.). Hence, these medical advancements have empowered patients and their families (proxies) with an important task of choosing their treatment preference during end-of-life care.[1]

"Decision-making" for end-of-life care has earned paramount importance as it has capability to prolong human life with the support of medical technologies or can let the natural death process continue by foregoing the treatment option.[2] Hence, end-of-life care is facing various ethical dilemmas. The purpose of this narrative review is to discuss issues such as autonomous decision making, importance of advance directives, rationing of care in futile treatments and costs involved in providing end-of-life care. This is a US centered study and the text does not necessarily apply to countries and contexts outside the United States.

Some Ethical Issues Surrounding End-of-Life Care

Autonomous Decision Making

"Decision making" is itself a very complex process of thoughts and sets-up various challenges for patients and their families to make up an end-of-life care decision.[3] Persons have a right to put forward their end-of-life treatment preferences. The Federal Patient Self-Determination Act (PSDA) effective since 1991 has facilitated communication between the healthcare providers and patients or consumers.[4] The person's right to autonomously voice their end-of-life treatment choices has to be respected ethically considering the use of advance treatments and their prognosis.

This right of autonomy has some limitations, and hence faces an ethical dilemma. The healthcare professional should respect the patient's autonomy while considering its limitation and carry out their duties to benefit the patient without doing harm.[5]

Even though we are discussing about patients right to autonomy we are talking about its limitations. To elaborate further, autonomy gives patients a right to control their treatment according to their preferences, though many a times their autonomy is not respected. They receive end-of-life care which is in-consistent with their end-of-life care preferences.[6] This gives importance to the ethical issue of autonomy surrounding end-of-life care preferences.

Physician's Role and Responsibilities to Resolve the Issue

Healthcare professionals can play an important role by providing detailed information about an advanced medical treatment which can be used during end-of-life care. Physicians can perform their duties rightfully by providing patients detailed information about the benefits, limitations and drawbacks of that treatment. Physician can work according to "deontological theory" and perform their duties to gain greatest good for the patient and act for patients benefit.[4] Even though the patient has autonomy to choose a treatment, physician can explain its implications and try to emphasize on its consequences. Here, the patient has to perform a self-beneficence duty to take an autonomous decision as a competent individual to undergo the treatment and prolong life or forgo a futile treatment for the greatest good of society by saving cost and emotional stress. If the patient insists to prolong life with medically advanced treatment intervention, which according to physician evaluation might be futile, physician has the upmost responsibility to explain the information facts about withholding or withdrawing the medical treatment and see to it that there is no unnecessary utilization of resources for the futile treatment without causing harm to the patient. Physicians should respect the beliefs and values of that patient before withholding or withdrawing a treatment or giving an order for DNR (do not resuscitate) or resuscitation. Physician, additionally has a duty to preserve patient's life but this duty is not to be confused with unnecessary use of resources and inflicting more harm than good to the patient by continuing medically futile treatments.[5]

Physicians have to reach a mutual agreement with the patient about withholding or withdrawing a futile treatment and explain the drawbacks of unrealistic expectations from the treatment. Communication between patient and families, discussing patient's goal regarding treatment and care, can be helpful to bridge a gap between the patient, their families and the physician.[6]

Advance Directives

An "advance directive" enables competent individuals to design and document their health care decision plan in advance in case of future disability or terminal illness. This advance directive can be of two types, instructional and proxy, which allow competent individuals to make their healthcare choices in advance or specify their wishes to their providers or families in case of future disability in carrying out end-of-life decision.[4] This can give the patient an "individual autonomy" so as to receive end-of-life care consistent with their preference. In case of a competent individual, he or she can convey or document their end-of-life treatment preferences autonomously to the authorities on admission or can take a consensus autonomous decision after getting end-of-life care information from the physician as discussed above.

On the other hand in case of incapacitated individuals, families play a central role as proxies or primary care givers. Families have a responsibility of putting forth the end-of-life care preference of the patient. Family members play the role of proxy due to the virtue of their relationship with the patient and may not be very good in guessing the patients preference for end-of-life decision making, in the case where explicit declaration of patients' preferences is not clear. These proxies try to judge the medical situation as the patient may have evaluated but it is seen that they are not very good at taking end-of-life decisions for the patients.

Families playing the crucial role of surrogate or proxy are emotionally attached to the incapacitated patient and hence their moral interest (emotional, financial pressure, etc.) may be diversified in opting for a treatment or declining them.[4] The unstable advance preferences may not be authentic in some eventful situations. Hence, the medical situation may need renewed evaluation and decision making. To address these ethical and legal issues arising from advance directives there is a need to educate the general population about the legal requirements and rights of the patient to accept or refuse a recommended treatment and advance directive. The information about proper implications and use of advance directives can facilitate in understanding and addressing legal issues arising from planning ahead by the patient or by the primary care givers.[4]

Rationing of Care and Futile Treatment

The technological advancements and innovations are reshaping the decisions and treatment preferences surrounding end-of-life care. These technologically advanced treatments have a capability to prolong the life of a patient rather than allowing the natural dying process. The end-of-life decisions to sustain life are considered on the basis of patient centered care, quality of life after these advance treatments and have to be weighed along with shared decision-making process.[1] These new medical treatments and technologies are increasing the number of people seeking long-term care. It is challenging to provide long-term advanced treatment and care to the population considering the increase in older population and assessing the projected increase in this population, especially when the baby boom (a cohort born between 1946–1964) reach old age by 2030.[4] It is assumed that people will adapt to healthy lifestyles and thus, this will reduce disabilities, diseases and injuries. This advancement will lower death rate and increase people living longer and needing long term care in their later life.[4]

People should understand that they are mortals and consider getting information and making plans for end-of-life care preferences.[7] The futile and expensive treatment at end-of-life situations are increasing the unaffordable cost of healthcare and promoting inequitable healthcare. The ethical value of patient autonomy and surrogate autonomy should be respected but weighed against the use of expensive treatment in futile case circumstances with current increase in healthcare costs. Hence, in case of futile treatments, families and patients can ethically consider the option for comfort care. The advanced technologies hold no promises for recovery. These treatments can also lead to few humiliating and undignified situations for the patients which can be emotionally burdensome. Healthcare rationing of end-of-life care in futile situations can be considered as greatest good for society but has to be weighed against the patient autonomy.[8]

It is difficult for the general population seeking medical care to understand the concept of limited treatment in case of futile cases. The stewardship of limiting medical care is surrounded by ethical issues as the patients and their families do not understand the need to limit treatment in some cases where it is futile. Healthcare providers and physicians are working towards this challenging task of making patients understand the need to refuse treatment as it may not benefit them and in some cases can cause harm.

"Bioethics" points this limiting treatment or refusing futile treatment option as "rationing of care" in cases where unanimous decision about refusing advance treatment is not made collaboratively by patient and their healthcare providers. There are no strict criteria to differentiate futile treatment; hence it has to be relied on expert judgment and case prognosis. Considering the aspect of access of quality care to the people who need them most, the rationing of care in futile situation can be justified. Rationing of care is present in the current healthcare system and can be justified as equitable justice if carried out ethically and equitably.[9] Medical resource allocation is often limited and hence has to be distributed equitably. There is a need for evaluating and assessing the medically advanced treatment so as to avoid any undue use of already limited resources. This can be achieved by good education, knowledge about advanced treatment implications and improved healthcare decision making from patients, their families and physicians.[7]

Costs Involved in End-of-Life Care

The expenditure on healthcare is too much in relation with total number of people and outcome. United States is spending a lot of money on health care and the average dollar amount per person is also much higher. Having said that, the health care expenditure is increasing, and at the same time people are spending more on getting the care they need. The cost of producing health care services due to advancement and innovations in technology is increasing the expenditure involved in providing these healthcare advanced treatment services. These healthcare services should not only target lengthening the life of people but also improve the quality of life,[10] especially when end-of-life decisions and the costs involved in it are concerned. Compassionate care is another option sought by the patients while considering end-of-life care which can be at times less costly and a good preference when medicine is unable to restore patient's health. The medical treatments are financially burdensome to some patients; hence easy accessibility to quality care at affordable cost can lessen the financial issue adherent to the end-of-life care considering the increase in the unaffordability of healthcare.[9]

Ethical Theories Involved in End-of-Life Care

Healthcare providers and physicians have to consider patient's perspective and preferences. They have to work against the egoistic theory by working for the good of the patient.[4] Patient's family members when implied with the task of making appropriate treatment choices or end-of-life care choices for the incapacitated patient should put aside their self-interest and judge the situation and come to a decision in the patient's best interest. This act of working towards achieving greatest good for the patient by family members and by the physician can be termed under "Virtue theory" of ethics.

Physicians have to judge the situation and provide appropriate treatment prognosis so that patients can make an autonomous choice of treatment preferences or patient's family can make these choices for them and work towards act of beneficence for the patient. While carrying out this act of beneficence, the physician has to provide information about the treatment, especially in case of futile treatment so as to avoid any undue harm to the patient. In case of futile treatments, healthcare providers also have to consider the allocation of limited resources available to manage the case scenario so as to avoid inequity. Hence, healthcare providers also have to consider the aspect of equitable and distributive justice in cases where expensive treatment provided to the patient during end-of-life situation may be futile, and utilize lot of resources, leading to unequal distribution of limited medical and technological resources.[4] Additionally, they have to address the issues of unnecessary and unequal distribution of resources by withdrawing or withholding the futile treatment.[5]

Policy Implications

The task of healthcare executives to manage ethical issues surrounding end-of-life care is challenging. Healthcare executives can address these ethical dilemmas ensuring certain policies to be followed during managing this task. They can guide the patients and their surrogates to make informed treatment preferences by providing them trustful information, appropriate prognosis and available options regarding the case specific treatment choices. They can assist the patient and their families to make a well judged end-of-life care decision and document their preferences. In case there is a disagreement between the healthcare provider and the patient or surrogate end-of-life care choices, then they can take appropriate steps by appointing an ethics committee to address this ethical or legal issue and document its proceedings. Healthcare executives can compile policies, so as to introduce, promote, and discuss the use of advanced directives as an admission procedure.[1] This can motivate the patients to make a living will (advanced directive) about their end-of-life care preferences which in due process can facilitate families to make appropriate decisions in case of incapacitated patients.

Healthcare organizations can work towards developing and implementing guidelines & policies for end-of-life care decision making, especially policies for withholding or withdrawing the treatment options so as to avoid the ethical dilemmas. There should be a proper disclosure mentioning the limitations of certain specific treatment options if there are any, so that the patients and families are well informed about their treatment options and make well-judged decisions. Healthcare executives can develop resources supporting palliative treatment care choices. They can additionally provide detailed information and knowledge about these palliative care options so as to facilitate patients and their families to make a competent end-of-life care preference. Healthcare organizations can provide effective support by appointing an interdisciplinary ethics committee and employee assistance facility available so as to address any ethical crisis.[1] A well-formed, consistent and integrated ethics committee can safeguard organization's future by increasing patient satisfaction, increasing organization's productivity, avoiding unethical activities, restricting undue costs, and reducing the risk of lawsuits.[11]

Conclusions and Future Implications

Healthcare providers should take an initiative and discuss patient's goal for end-of-life care or palliative care, as their preferences can change from person to person. Some patients might target for cure or some for comfort care, hence this trustful communication can avoid the ethical crisis surrounding that topic. The stability of these health preference goals is another issue as it has a potentiality to change with illness. Hence, the health scenario in each specific case has to be renewably evaluated so as to opt for scenario-based preferences. Here, the role played by clinicians is important as they can promote communication, education and discussion related to end-of-life care preferences and their implications among the patient, and their families in order to facilitate improved decision making. Effective advance planning or advanced directives can assist in putting forth patient's autonomous choices but flexibility in these advanced directives can be appraised as it can accommodate any inadvertent scenario-based preference change and evaluation.

Community standards can work well where the patient's desire from the end-of-life treatment choices is not well demarcated.[3] It is crucial to have a public dialogue discussing the ethical issues and dilemmas surrounding end-of-life care. This open discussion can facilitate development and implementation of policies and guidelines safeguarding the interest of patients and healthcare organizations.[1] Much progress has been made to address the ethical issues surrounding end-of-life care situation, and with the continued advancement in medical science, and its leading role in our lives demands further research into this topic. As age advances so thus the illness in many cases, hence there is a need to research and implement recommendations to relieve the stress faced by people during that critical time and optimize quality care to improve and ease end-of-life journey.[3]

Endnotes

1. American College of Healthcare Executives (ACHE) Decisions Near the End of Life. [(accessed on 2 March 2016)]. Available online: https://www.ache.org/policy/endoflif. cfm.
2. Meisel A. From Birth to Death and Bench to Clinic: The Hastings Center Bioethics Briefing Book for Journalists, Policymakers, and Campaigns. In: Crowley M., editor. *End-of-Life Care*. Garrison The Hastings Center; Garrison, NY, USA: 2008, pp. 51–54.
3. Emanuel L., Scandrett K. Decisions at the End of Life: Have We Come of Age? BMC Med. 2010 doi: 10.1186/1741-7015-8-57.
4. Morrison E.E. *Health Care Ethics: Critical Issues for 21st Century*. 2nd ed. Jones and Bartlett; Sudbury, MA, USA: 2009.
5. Thorns A. Ethical and Legal Issues in End-of-Life Care. Clin. Med. 2010;10:282–285. doi: 10.7861/clinmedicine.10-3-282.
6. Winzelberg G., Hanson L., Tulsky J. Beyond Autonomy: Diversifying End-of-Life Decision-Making Approaches to Serve Patients and Families. J. Am. Geriatr. Soc. 2005;53:1046–1050. doi: 10.1111/j.1532-5415.2005.53317.x.
7. PBS NEWSHOUR Debating Ethics of Rationing End-of-Life Care. [(accessed on 9 March 2016)]. Available online: http://www.pbs.org/newshour/bb/health/jan-june10/miller_04-26.html.
8. John Hopkins Medicine Reasoning Through the Rationing of End-of-Life Care. [(accessed on 8 March 2016)]. Available online: http://www.hopkinsmedicine.org/news/media/releases/Reasoning_Through_The_Rationing_Of_EndOfLife_Care.

9. Baily M. Futility, Autonomy, and Cost in End-of-Life Care. J. Law Med. Ethics. 2011;39:172–182. doi: 10.1111/j.1748-720X.2011.00586.x.

10. Healthy People 2020. [(accessed on 8 March 2016)]; Available online: https://www.healthypeople.gov/2020/about/foundation-health-measures/Health-Related-Quality-of-Life-and-Well-Being.

11. Caulfield S.E. Health Care Facility Ethics Committees: New Issues in the Age of Transparency. [(accessed on 8 March 2016)]. Available online: http://www.americanbar.org/publications/human_rights_magazine_home/human_rights_vol34_2007/fall2007/hr_fall07_caulfi.html.

Hospice Is Still a Mystery to Many

Paula Spencer Scott

Most people do not understand what hospice is or how it works. Many are even afraid of the idea. In the following viewpoint, Paula Spencer Scott explains what hospice is and addresses many of the common fears and issues that surround it. She also explains how hospice care can make the end of a patient's life calmer and easier, as the patient does not have to spend his or her final days in a hospital setting. Hospice is becoming more accepted in western nations. Scott is the author of Surviving Alzheimer's: Practical Tips and Soul-Saving Wisdom for Caregivers. *Her work has appeared in* Woman's Day, WebMD *and* Parenting.

As you read, consider the following questions:

1. What are some of the misunderstandings concerning what hospice care is?
2. Is hospice something that a patient has to continue, even if they don't like it?
3. How does hospice continue after the patient's death?

An interesting thing happens when Dawn Gross brings up hospice to patients or their families:

"Oh, no, we don't want that!" they often say.

"OK," says Gross, a hospice and palliative care physician in San Francisco. "Tell me exactly what you don't want, so we're sure not to give you that."

Going off to some facility, they tell her. Losing control of care. Being knocked out by morphine. Or—the clincher—giving up. When Gross assures them that hospice isn't at all like that—that two-thirds of hospice care takes place in the person's home or a long-term care facility, that the patient can still receive medical care, and that Medicare and most private health insurers pay for it in full—they often change their minds.

In 2011, about a million people died in hospice—about 42 percent of all those who died, according to the National Hospice and Palliative Care Organization in Alexandria, Va.—and its use is growing.

Still, misconceptions about this end-of-life service abound. As a result, many who might benefit from hospice don't sign up until the very end: About a third of hospice users enroll for less than a week, and the median time is 18 days.

So how can you tell whether hospice is the right choice for you or your loved one? The answer depends on what you believe hospice is, your current goals, and what you think it can—or can't—do for you.

Here's what you need to know.

Hospice Is a Philosophy of Care, Not a Brick-and-Mortar Location.

Most people say they want to die at home, but only about 1 in 4 end up doing so. One big reason: It's often just too hard. "Trying to care for someone with a serious illness, especially at home, without hospice is like trying to have surgery without anesthesia," says Ira Byock, the executive director of the Providence Institute for Human Caring.

Hospices bring everything you might need to the home—hospital bed, bedside commode, medications, bandages, expert consults—tailored to your needs.

But if you're daunted by home care, or simply don't want a loved one to die in your home, hospice care also is available in facilities and hospitals.

Signing Up Doesn't Mean Giving Up All Medical Care.

Transitioning to hospice means shifting from one set of goals (how to get longer life through a cure) to another (how to get the best quality of life out of whatever time is left).

"When people say, 'I don't want to give up,' the key is to understand what they think they're giving up," Gross says. Even when a cure is no longer viable, therapies that improve symptoms and raise comfort can continue. "I deliver very aggressive care in hospice," she adds.

If, however, you feel that you have not exhausted all of your treatment options in search of a cure, hospice may not be for you. Medicare hospice rules require forgoing curative treatments.

That may soon change, though. In July, Medicare announced the expansion of a five-year pilot program to 141 hospices in 40 states to allow patients to continue pursuing curative treatments while under hospice care.

You Have to Qualify for Hospice, but You Can Opt Out at Any Time.

To qualify for hospice benefits, either through Medicare or private insurance, two physicians must certify that you have a life-altering condition with an expected prognosis of six months or less. This time frame is arbitrary, however; there's no biological or scientific basis for knowing how long you have left, Gross says.

If You Start Hospice and Realize It's Not for You, You Can Quit.

How can you know when to try hospice? This should be part of ongoing discussions with your health care team, Byock says— "ongoing" because goals and needs evolve.

You May Live Longer During the Time You Have Left.

Hospice recipients live longer, on average, than those receiving standard care, research shows. A 2010 study of lung cancer patients found they lived nearly three months longer; another study, looking at the most common terminal diagnoses, found the same, ranging from an average of 20 more days (gallbladder cancer) to 69 days (breast cancer).

You Can Still See Your Regular Doctor.

Multidisciplinary by intention, a basic hospice team consists of a physician and nurse (both on call 24 hours a day); a social worker, counselor or chaplain; and a volunteer. Many hospices offer added services: psychologists, psychiatrists, home health aides, art or pet therapists, nutritionists, and occupational, speech, massage or physical therapists. You may also continue to see your regular doctor. And you remain in charge of your medical decisions.

The Goal of Pain Management in Hospice Is to Enable You to Live Well—Not Sedate You.

"People often mistakenly think pain medicine will make the person sleepy to the point where they can't interact," says Karen Whitley Bell, a hospice nurse for 20 years and author of *Living at the End of Life*. "To the contrary, if you live with pain unnecessarily, it makes you more tired and irritable, and robs you of quality of life." When drugs like morphine are used, it's to treat anxiety and to lessen pain, which has been shown to be undertreated at the end of life—not hasten death, as many people mistakenly believe.

Hospice Can Enrich, and Sometimes Salvage, the Last Stage of Life.

Almost a third of those with a terminal illness die in the hospital, hooked up to machines that do little to halt the process of dying. Hospice is designed to support the more personal aspects of this life stage: reflecting on one's legacy and life meaning, focusing on relationships in a deeper and more intentional way, achieving a sense of closure, and realizing any end-of-life goals, such as attending a grandchild's graduation or getting financial affairs in order.

Hospice Is for the Entire Family.

It's not always easy to witness the hallucinations of delirium or understand the body language of someone who can no longer speak, for example. A hospice nurse can help interpret what's happening, or explain the signs of imminent death. And when families need a break, the sick person can spend up to five days at a time in inpatient respite care, such as in a nursing home or hospice facility.

Hospice Continues After Death.

Many people don't realize that optional follow-up grief support for 12 months is included under Medicare rules. "For many of our families, their journey with hospice is only beginning once their loved one dies," says bereavement counselor Anne Alesch. She runs separate support groups for surviving spouses and adult children.

Ultimately, hospice makes space for "the spirit, the love and the quieting of the mind" that tend to take precedence as the body prepares to shut down, says Nina Angela McKissock, author of *From Sun to Sun: A Hospice Nurse Reflects on the Art of Dying.* Adds Ira Byock: "We make a mistake in assuming that serious illness and dying are mostly medical. They're fundamentally personal."

More On Hospices

As hospice has evolved from a grassroots movement to a booming industry, a few bad apples have inevitably emerged. What should you look for when evaluating a hospice? "There's no easy shortcut to evaluating quality care," says Joe Rotella, M.D., chief medical director of the American Academy of Hospice and Palliative Medicine. But here are some questions to ask.

Is the Hospice Accredited?

"Hospices aren't required to be certified or accredited, but those that seek outside accreditation are making a special commitment to quality care," Rotella says. The Joint Commission, Community Health Accreditation Partner, the National Hospice and Palliative Care Organization and other groups have created standards of excellence that participating hospices must meet. Some state agencies also certify hospices.

Has the Hospice Been Surveyed by a State or Federal Oversight Organization? If so, When? What Were the Results?

The Affordable Care Act now requires hospices that accept Medicare—almost all of them—to complete surveys and provide data about several quality measures, including how well they manage patients' pain. Eventually the results will be publicly available online. For now, ask if a survey has been done and what the results show.

Is the Medical Director Board-Certified?

Board certification is not a requisite, "but having a medical director who is certified by a medical board as a palliative medicine specialist offers one more assurance of training, experience and overall quality," Rotella says.

How Many Patients Does the Hospice Program Care For?

Hospices come in many sizes. Although smaller ones may provide more personalized care, larger ones (those serving at least 100 patients) have more resources.

What Is the Typical Caseload?

Ideally, a hospice nurse or nurse practitioner should manage a caseload with no more than 12 patients.

Periodical and Internet Sources Bibliography

The following articles have been selected to supplement the diverse views presented in this chapter.

Katherine Clark and Jane Phillips, "End of Life Care: The Importance of Culture and Ethnicity." Focus: Culture and Diversity. http:// palliativecare.issuelab.org/resources/17334/17334.pdf.

Mikaela Conley, "Parents Fight Canadian Hospital for Child's Survival." ABC News, March 10, 2011. https://abcnews.go.com/ Health/baby-josephs-treatment-sparks-controversy-pediatric-end-life/story?id=13032001.

Elizabeth Craig and Margaret Ratcliff, "Controversies in Correctional End-of-Life Care." *Journal of Correctional Health Care*, July 1, 2002. http://journals.sagepub.com/doi/ abs/10.1177/107834580200900206?journalCode=jcxa.

Kathrina Jeorgette Flores, "End-of-Life Care and the Physician-Assisted Suicide Debate." Modern Medicine Network, July 1, 2016. http://www.physicianspractice.com/career/end-life-care-and-physician-assisted-suicide-debate.

The Gainesville Sun, "End-of-Life Choices Are a Topic Swirling in Political Controversy." September 16, 2014. http://www. gainesville.com/news/20140916/editorial-end-of-life-debate.

Howard Gleckman, "The Real Story Behind the Latest Hospice Controversy." *Forbes*, January 3, 2014. https://www.forbes.com/ sites/howardgleckman/2014/01/03/the-real-story-behind-the-latest-hospice-controversy/#4ef275504e78.

Sarah Kliff, "Medicare Wants to Pay Doctors to Talk about Death. Expect political controversy." *Vox*, July 8, 2015. https://www.vox. com/2015/7/8/8915841/medicare-end-of-life.

Jessica Marcy, "Doctors See Benefit in End-of-Life Controversy." NBC News, August 14, 2009. http://www.nbcnews.com/id/32418642/ ns/health-health_care/t/doctors-see-benefit-end-of-life-controversy/#.WwA4XEgvw2w.

Timothy Quill, MD, and John Mitchell, "Palliative Care: A Closer Look into the Controversy of Assisted Suicide." Patient Power, November 12, 2007. https://www.patientpower.info/audio/palliative-care-a-closer-look-into-the-controversy-of-assisted-suicide.

Mildred Z. Solomon, Deborah E. Sellers, Karen S. Heller, Deborah L. Dokken, Marcia Levetown, Cynda Rushton, Robert D. Truog, Alan R. Fleischman, "New and Lingering Controversies in Pediatric End-of-Life Care." *Pediatrics*, October 2005, VOLUME 116 / ISSUE 4. http://pediatrics.aappublications.org/content/116/4/872.short.

Sharon Valente, PhD, RN & Bill Haley, PhD, "Culturally Diverse Communities and End-of-Life Care." American Psychological Association. http://www.apa.org/pi/aging/programs/eol/end-of-life-diversity.aspx.

GLOBALVIEWPOINTS

CHAPTER 2

How We Are Laid to Rest

The Burning Question

Thomas Laqueur

In the following viewpoint, excerpted for length, Thomas Laqueur presents a history of the use of cremation in burials and makes the argument that the decision to be cremated is one of the last decisions that people make to express their wishes. The author brings the subject into the present day with examples of how people are still using cremation, and the decisions that surround it, as their final self-expressive act. Laqueur is professor of history at the University of California, Berkeley and author of The Work of the Dead: A Cultural History of Mortal Remains *(Princeton University Press, 2015).*

As you read, consider the following questions:

1. How might Christianity have affected the practice of cremation?
2. Why did Ferdinando Coletti think that having a relative's ashes in the home could be a good thing?
3. Why did evangelical churches oppose burning the dead?

C remation of the dead was the norm in the first century AD and the exception by the fourth. No one has explained why, although everyone agrees that it was not, as was long thought, due to the rise of Christianity. It is true that some early Christians had objections to cremation, and that their pagan opponents associated their strange Christian belief in resurrection with a need to put the dead body into the ground. But there were no theological grounds to believe that the prospects of a happy afterlife had anything to do with whether a body was burned or buried, or eaten by a lion. Besides, the new religion was too small to have had so great an influence on funerary practices so early on.

By the time of Charlemagne, in the ninth century, inhumation had become the mark of the Christian way of disposing of the dead, and cremation was associated with the pagans. The emperor insisted that the newly Christianised Germanic tribes abandon their fiery pyres. By the 11th century, in all of Europe—and much earlier in some places—the only proper place for a dead body was in a churchyard. Exclusion from burial in sacred ground and from priestly rites was understood as the most terrible consequence of excommunication or suicide. Only heretics, witches and other miscreants of the worst sort were burned—alive, not dead—and their ashes scattered, to symbolise the eradication of the evil they represented.

It made no difference to the first 18th-century proponents of cremation how and why the world of antiquity gave up burial. For more than a millennium it had been the Christian way of caring for the dead body. Fire and ash thus took their place on the frontline of the culture. The embracing of cremation again in the 18th and 19th centuries was a way of honouring the classical world and rejecting the new one that had supplanted it. Frederick the Great, always ready to show his philosophical hand, supposedly asked that he be "burned in the Roman fashion." Of course, that didn't happen; he even failed to be buried as he had wanted—with his dogs, in the grounds of Sanssouci. But one of his aunts fared better: in 1752, she was cremated "for aesthetic reasons." It may have been the first documented cremation in the West in modern history.

Cremation in its neoclassical inflection was on the side of progress in the sense of a return to a long-gone and better time. But it was not necessarily on the side of revolution, secularism, materialism and the new cult of reason. Jacob Grimm, the philologist and collector of fairytales, in his address to the Berlin Academy in 1849, made the case that the advent of cremation in preclassical antiquity had represented a step forward in the spiritual or mental cultivation of a people: the use of fire distinguished humans from animals. He argued that it coincided with the advent of religion: spiritlike fire rises to heaven, whereas flesh is earthbound; burnt sacrifices were a way of connecting humans and the gods. Broadly speaking, there were "aesthetic merits of a fiery grave." But cremation is practical as well, Grimm continued: ashes are easier to transport. And it is rational: fire does quickly what earth does slowly. Finally, he said simply, to burn the dead was to honour antiquity. In other words, cremation is on the side of progress. But he did not go on to draw the conclusion, as others would, that burial—dank, morbid, the quintessence of baroque darkness—is therefore retrograde. Nor did he think that a return to ancient practices would be easy: burial was too embedded in the Christian symbolic system of the sleeping dead, and their eventual rising into a life everlasting, for that.

In 1794, burning the dead took on new meaning. After 1,000 years in which all the dead—excluding heretics—were buried, Jacobin revolutionaries in France reintroduced public cremation to Europe: an explicitly public alternative to Christian burial. More precisely, they produced the first full-scale, Roman republic–style cremation in almost 2,000 years, and the first cremation of any sort in France for 1,000.

The 18th-century body in question was that of Charles Nicolas Beauvais de Préau, a doctor, member of the national assembly from the department of the Seine, and, at the time of his death, the representative of the Convention to the politically divided city of Toulon. After a royalist takeover, he was put in prison; there he fell mortally ill. When Toulon was retaken by the armies of the Convention in late December 1793—the siege of Toulon was one of Napoleon's first great moments—De Préau was too sick to travel back to Paris and was moved instead to Montpellier. There he died, on 28 March 1794.

The following day, the revolutionary municipal government reinvented cremation: the body of this "martyr of liberty would be cremated in a civil ceremony," it announced, "and his ashes gathered in an urn which would be conveyed to the Convention" in Paris. In what is almost an act of historical enactment, De Préau's body was laid on an old-fashioned wood-fuelled pyre, which might have been seen in *The Iliad* or the Rome of Cato. The flames took all day, and well into the night, to consume the body. The next morning, the ashes were collected and taken first to the local Temple of Reason—the site since 1793 of the explicitly anti-Christian Cult of Reason and its festivals—and from there sent on to the capital, to be ensconced in the national archives.

The link between cremation, on the one hand, and support for an alternative to Christianity (that is, the Cult of Reason), on the other, became even more explicit when the law of 21 Brumaire in the year IV made cremation legal on 11 November 1795. Its political bite was clear: "Whereas the greater part of the people in antiquity burnt their dead," begins the decree, and whereas "this practice was abolished, or in any case fell into disuse, only because of religious influences"—read Christianity—it would now become available again as part of an effort to create a new national cult of the dead and to discredit the old one.

Never mind that the law of 21 Brumaire got its history wrong: Christianity had not caused the decline of Roman cremation. The fact that men of the Enlightenment and revolution believed that it had was enough to make reinstating cremation both an anticlerical protest and a neoclassical alternative to long-established practice. It also set the stage for the battles of the next century.

In 1796, the Convention solicited ideas for the reform of funeral rites, intended to make them less dependent on the church. Père-Lachaise, the new kind of space for the dead, was a product of this cultural ferment; many harebrained schemes that were suggested came to nothing. Cremation stood in between. Having been made legal—or rather, having entered the cognisance of civil law—for the first time in Europe in 1796, as part of the cultural reform programme of the Directory, it could be made illegal when political winds shifted. The Third Republic made cremation legal again in 1889: the *laicisation* of the dead.

At issue in all this was not a particular view of the consequences of cremation versus burial; cleanliness, which loomed so large in later debates and in contemporary arguments for closing churchyards, played almost no part. Nor did materialist philosophy—there was no interest in technology. Cremation was meant to strike a blow at a 1,000-year-old community of the dead buried in sacred ground, and to offer a historically based alternative. The reasons the church opposed it are clear. But even Louis-Sébastien Mercier, the dramatist who opposed cremation on ecological grounds, disliked it for aesthetic and sociological reasons: the pyres were hateful; the flames were cadaverous; and the private sepulchres made possible by having one's dead grandfather and uncle in urns that could be put in the cupboard were "an affront to the calm and repose of society."

Later, the same image was used to make the opposite case. Ferdinando Coletti, a distinguished Italian medical academic and liberal reformer, reflected on the French experience. Having the urns of one's relatives at home would exercise "a very healthy influence on the morality of the individual"; they would become a "sanctuary of the family, which is the eternal base of social order." This makes a would-be collection of ashes seem like a Chinese ancestral altar. The remains of the dead call the living to imagine a moral order.

In the first few decades of modern cremation—from the 1870s to the late 1890s—the necrogeography of ashes mattered less than the process of making them in the first place. Recreating the republican funeral pyres of antiquity was associated with revolutionary anti-clericalism and neoclassicism. Employing hi-tech methods married that pedigree to progress, materialism and reason.

Nowhere was cremation more politically and religiously charged than in Italy. The Italian pioneers of cremation were doctors, scientists, progressives, Positivists; they were republicans and supporters of the Risorgimento; they were anti-clerical. Most important—or rather, representing all these ills, from the perspective of the church—they were Freemasons. For religious conservatives, Masonry connected the French revolution and all its sins with the rebirth of cremation in the second half of the 19th century. The pope had condemned it first in 1738, and did so again many times after that. More pointedly, the Abbé Barruel's widely translated and immensely influential history of Jacobinism argued that the revolution itself could be summed up as a Masonic conspiracy: "what evil is there not to be feared" from them, "deists, atheists, sceptics," begetters of "Liberty and Equality," plotters all?

The Masonic lodges of Italy, especially of Milan and Turin, provided an institutional infrastructure for the advocacy of cremation, as well as for the invention of new rituals and for construction of purpose-built crematoria. Jacob Salvatore Morelli, one of the main early publicists for cremation, was a freethinker, feminist, campaigner for more liberal divorce laws, and a Mason. The minister of the interior who gave permission for the first legal cremation in Italy, on 22 January 1876, was a Freemason, and so was Alberto Keller, the German Lutheran businessman who was cremated. He had died two years earlier and been embalmed, in the hope that when technology reached an advanced enough stage he could be cremated. Before a great concourse of worthies, and in an up-to-date crematorium modelled on a Roman temple, Keller finally got his wish. His ashes were placed in a tomb that he had had built in the Protestant part of Milan's municipal cemetery. There, according to the *New York Times*, it was visited by "great numbers of Milanese who are desirous of looking upon the ashes of one who had been the originator of an epoch in the civilised world."

Giuseppe Garibaldi, representative of populist democratic nationalism in the wars that led to a united Italy—and a Masonic grand master—wanted to be cremated, too. For him it would be one last blow against the clerical establishment whose hold on the dead, he thought, was the foundation of its power. He wanted to go in the style of republican Rome, and had no interest in proving the hygienic virtues of the technologically advanced furnace, or in the politics of funeral reform. The great man had left his widow precise instructions for the size of the old-fashioned pyre (no modern coke or gas oven for him), the kind of wood to be used, and the disposal of his ashes: they were to be put in an urn and placed near his daughters' graves.

Like a Roman gentleman, he wanted to rest with his family. The ceremony was to take place privately, and before his death was announced.

But no one was interested in following Garibaldi's wishes. Burning him on a Roman pyre would clearly be a snub to the church. When he died, in 1882, cremation was legal only under special circumstances. The so-called Crispi Laws of 1888—named after Francesco Crispi, the Garibaldian, decidedly leftist, strongly anti-clerical Italian prime minister—made cremation generally legal and mandated access to ashes to state-supervised cemeteries. As for the rest of Garibaldi's wishes, they represented, to almost everyone, the hero's posthumous refusal of one last public service to the secular state. No one was for it, not even the cremation societies, which distanced themselves from the young widow. In the end, Garibaldi went to his grave with great civic pomp; his dead body lying in wait for six weeks while his followers quarrelled.

The church forbade membership of cremation societies and the demanding of cremation for oneself or for others—not as acts contrary to dogma, but as acts hostile to the church. Missionaries were never to condone the practice, but they could baptise high-caste Hindus on their deathbeds, even if they knew that they would have wished to be cremated. Meanwhile, a conservative Catholic journal understood cremation as hubris. The deceased "orders that his body become not dust, but ashes. It is he himself who imposes this destruction, not God ... [He] escapes God's authority and the duty to submit to him." Death, it reminded readers, was inflicted on mankind to punish sin. Cremation was a show of human power in the face of death, a gesture at mastering the dead, even if mortality itself could not be mastered. Cremation self-consciously represented—much more than the cemetery had—the disruption of a cult of memory that Christianity had helped create and sustain. The author of the 1908 *Catholic Encyclopedia* summed up the case: cremation was making a "public profession of irreligion and materialism." And so it was with variations elsewhere on the continent.

In Germany, the impetus for cremation came not from Freemasons' lodges but from municipal and military doctors (advocates of hygiene), from working-class movements, and from others who wanted to align themselves with progress, with the forward march of history defined in a number of ways. The fact that some of the 19th century's most hardline radical materialists—Moleschott and Vogt, among others—embraced cremation helped make it attractive to many on the left. In 1920, when one might think more consequential matters were at hand, a small debate took place between German communists and social democrats about whether members of cremation societies should be obliged to remove their children from religious instruction in public schools. Yes, argued the communists, because at stake was cultural revolution; half steps were not enough.

And indeed they weren't when the Bolsheviks came to power in Russia. They very quickly took up the cause of cremation because it was both practical and scientific ("Side by side with the car, tractor, and electrification—make way for cremation," read one poster), because it was a rejection of religion, and, perhaps most important, because it seemed to offer an alternative to the dangerous space of the cemetery, where citizens might create communities outside the socialist sphere. In 1927, the new revolutionary Russian cremation society would identify itself unabashedly as "militantly Godless." The first crematorium in Moscow was built in 1927, on the site of the great Donskoi monastery, technology on the site of the old religion. (A pit within its walls would hold the ashes of cremated victims of Stalin's purges.)

Socialists in Germany also aligned modern cremation with their freedom-loving ancestors who had burned their dead in the primeval forests. Progress was rooted in nostalgia. Those with "an ardent zeal for progress ... might not be sorry to find from the records of history ... that with the Teutonic race also cremation was once the ruling custom," wrote Karl Blind, the German revolutionary and member of Marx's circle since 1848 days.

Half a century earlier, the philosopher Johann Gottlieb Fichte (1762–1814) had a strange utopian vision of Germany in the 22nd century, in which burning the dead had become a unifying ritual. Populist, free from aristocracy, and nationalist, the Christian churches in this Germany had all agreed among themselves to cremate their dead: the ashes of a soldier who had fallen in battle would be put in an urn and sent back to a sepulchre in his hometown, where it would be placed—along with his name—on the highest shelf; on a rung below would be the urns of those who had counselled the state wisely; then those of good householders, men and women, and their good children, all identified by name. On the lowest level would come the nameless, presumably those not brave, nor wise, nor good. Through this intensely local and intimate columbarium, Fichte was able to envision a new community of the dead, defined not by the churchyard or by old hierarchies, but by service to home, heart and nation.

Whichever appreciative interpretation of cremation one adopted in Germany, or elsewhere on the continent, the alternative was always clear: religious custom. Evangelical churches opposed the burning of the dead because of its association with socialism and radical materialism, its general disregard for religion, and its seeming lack of interest in communities of the dead rendered into ashes. In the Catholic south it was unthinkable. Priests were forbidden to give last rites to those who had asked that their bodies be cremated; ashes were excluded from burial in church cemeteries. It was beyond the pale. There could be no doubt what the mass membership of working-class socialists—not just in Germany, but in the Netherlands and Austria—signified.

For almost all Jewish authorities, cremation meant the same thing: apostasy. There were a few exceptions to the almost total rabbinic condemnation. When the chief rabbi of Rome, Hayim (Vittorio) Castiglioni, died in 1911, he was cremated and his ashes buried in the Jewish cemetery in Trieste. A Reform rabbi in the United States argued in 1891 that cremation was practised by the ancient people of Israel and it had fallen into abeyance only for practical or contingent reasons: wood was expensive, and burning bodies had become associated with execution at the stake, and thus had horrible associations. Modern cremation, on the other hand, was aesthetically attractive and avoided "the slow, loathsome dissolution of the body in a pit," with all the attendant poisons in the air and water, and all the dangers to health that these created. Even most of his Reform colleagues demurred. And in Europe, the only real question was not whether it was lawful to cremate—the answer was no—but whether the ashes could be buried in a Jewish cemetery. This in turn raised a number of religious-legal issues. Were ashes a dead body? If so, were they ritually impure, and hence did they need to be dealt with properly? Did they require burial as did other bodies, no matter how sinful the deceased had been in asking to be cremated?

The resolution of the cremation question varied from place to place. The British burial society condemned cremation but permitted ritual care of the dead and burial in Jewish cemeteries; some rabbis in Germany allowed burial and prayers, but would not themselves see the body to the grave. In general, cremation emerged as a symbolically defining issue for modern Jewish communities in the late 19th and early 20th centuries, and even more so after the Holocaust, a new litmus test for how far one could deviate from historical practices and remain Jewish. An astonishing percentage opted for modernity: in Frankfurt, Dresden, Hamburg, Nuremberg and Stuttgart, in Turin and Bologna, a higher proportion of Jews were cremated than were Protestants. Significant numbers chose cremation in Budapest and Vienna, too. Perhaps the Holocaust changed the calculus. (Although 10% of Israeli Jews today claim they want to be cremated, fewer than 100 availed themselves of Israel's only crematorium, which opened in 2005 and was burned down by arsonists two years later.)

In Britain, neither anti-clericalism—battles over church rates and access to churchyards were essentially over—nor a strong revolutionary tradition, nor an explicit commitment to materialism had much to do with the advent of cremation. The organised working class was indifferent, if not affirmatively hostile, to it. The tone was set in 1874, by what a local newspaper called an "exciting demonstration" by women, from the humbler parts of town, against a motion before the West Hartlepool Improvement Commissioners. Instead of burning the dead—a "revolting idea"—the commissioners should spend their time providing "suitable burial-ground for their decent interment."

The Labour party, unlike continental socialist parties, never took up the cause of cremation. Perhaps hostility to the Anatomy Act went too deep; smoke in a poorhouse chimney signalled a pauper body not decently buried. No writer in Britain was quite as outspoken as the widely read American freethinker Augustus Cobb, who saw in the history of burial the heavy hand of benighted clerisy: "by adroit management [the grave] became a connecting link between things seen and unseen, and was the most potent factor that the church possessed for retaining its hold over its prostrate votaries," he wrote. Edward Gibbon had it right, Cobb thought, when in *The Decline and Fall of the Roman Empire* he scoffed at the late-imperial emperors, generals and consuls who, out of "superstitious reverence," "devoutly visited the sepulchres of a tent maker and a fisherman."

Cremation in the 19th and early 20th centuries was the cause of the cultural avant garde, the professional upper middle class allied with a sprinkling of aristocrats (the dukes of Bedford and Westminster, for example), hygiene specialists, Freemasons, eccentrics of various sorts—it was a Welsh Druid who legalised cremation—religious progressives, spiritualists and Romantic socialists such as Robert Blatchford, the Fabian follower of William

Morris, who loved Sir Thomas Browne's Urne-Buriall because it evoked a layered English deep time: archaeological remains of an ancestral and communal past. Set beside the bracing discourse of cleanliness, ecological efficiency, expertise and progress— cremation as a force in world history—there was in Britain a sense that it was also a way to allow everyone to imagine and care for their dead as they wished.

It gradually became acceptable, if not yet widespread. The first burial of cremated remains in Westminster Abbey was in 1905, 20 years after cremation became legal; that year, 99.9% of British men and women who died were buried. By the late 1960s, for the first time, more than half the dead in the UK were cremated; today, the proportion is around 70%. In the US the idea of cremation lost its strangeness more precipitously: in 1960, fewer than 4% of bodies were cremated; today the figure is around 44%.

But as cremation has become more commonplace and unremarkable, it has also enabled new and wildly creative ways in which the living can abide with the dead. There are precedents. In the fourth century BC, the wife—also his sister—of King Mausolus of Halicarnassus loved him so much that not only did she build him a great tomb—the first mausoleum, and a wonder of the ancient world—she also ingested some of his ashes so that he would live within her.

Today there are endless possibilities. In rural Virginia a hunter I knew told me that he and his buddies took some of the ashes of a dead friend, loaded them in the black powder shells that he had made, and shot them into the forest air. The rest they put on a salt lick near their hunting cabin, so that the ashes could be ingested by the deer they might kill and eat some time in the future. (I am sure they came up with the first of these rituals themselves, and had not read about Hunter S Thompson's funeral in 2005, when his ashes, along with red, white, blue and green fireworks, were fired into the air from a cannon.)

One woman told me that her grandmother's ashes coloured the ink that she used for her tattoos; another, who had divorced her husband in large part because he was more interested in sex with himself than with her, that she had put his ashes next to a jar of Vaseline in her bathroom. The family of a professional photographer put his ashes into 35mm film cartridges and buried these all over the world, in places where he had worked.

It still matters in some circles today—as it did for those who revived cremation in the late 18th and 19th centuries—how we live with the dead.

Burial Practices Are Windows to the Way a Culture Lives

James Michael Dorsey

In the following viewpoint James Michael Dorsey describes ten very different burial ceremonies from all over the world, which are quite different from the traditional burial ceremonies in the United States and other Western countries. Dorsey is an explorer, author and photographer who has traveled off the beaten path in 35 countries. He lives among indigenous peoples and records their cultures. His work has appeared in Christian Science Monitor, BBC Wildlife, WEND, Sea Kayaker, *and* TravelersTales.

As you read, consider the following questions:

1. What does the author mean when he says, "Burial practices are windows to a culture that speak volumes about how it lives"?
2. What are the similarities between an air sacrifice and a sky burial? Why might they have been used, besides as a religious ritual?
3. Why is fire so important to burial in Bali?

T he modern dictionary defines the word 'burial' as placing a body in the ground.

But burying the deceased was not always the case.

Just as primitive man has long worshiped the four elements

of Earth, Sky, Water, and Fire, so too have these elements taken their place in burial practices as diverse as the different tribes of the earth.

The way mankind deals with its dead says a great deal about those left to carry on. Burial practices are windows to a culture that speak volumes about how it lives.

As we are told in Genesis, man comes from dust, and returns to it. We have found many different ways to return. Here are 10 that I found particularly fascinating:

Air Sacrifice—Mongolia

Lamas direct the entire ceremony, with their number determined by the social standing of the deceased. They decide the direction the entourage will travel with the body, to the specific day and time the ceremony can happen.

Mongolians believe in the return of the soul. Therefore the lamas pray and offer food to keep evil spirits away and to protect the remaining family. They also place blue stones in the dead person's bed to prevent evil spirits from entering it.

No one but a lama is allowed to touch the corpse, and a white silk veil is placed over the face. The naked body is flanked by men on the right side of the yurt while women are placed on the left. Both have their respective right or left hand placed under their heads, and are situated in the fetal position.

The family burns incense and leaves food out to feed all visiting spirits. When time comes to remove the body, it must be passed through a window or a hole cut in the wall to prevent evil from slipping in while the door is open.

The body is taken away from the village and laid on the open ground. A stone outline is placed around it, and then the village dogs that have been penned up and not fed for days are released to consume the remains. What is left goes to the local predators.

The stone outline remains as a reminder of the person. If any step of the ceremony is left out, no matter how trivial, bad karma is believed to ensue.

Sky Burial—Tibet

This is similar to the Mongolian ceremony. The deceased is dismembered by a rogyapa, or body breaker, and left outside away from any occupied dwellings to be consumed by nature.

To the western mind, this may seem barbaric, as it did to the Chinese who outlawed the practice after taking control of the country in the 1950s. But in Buddhist Tibet, it makes perfect sense. The ceremony represents the perfect Buddhist act, known as Jhator. The worthless body provides sustenance to the birds of prey that are the primary consumers of its flesh.

To a Buddhist, the body is but an empty shell, worthless after the spirit has departed. Most of the country is surrounded by snowy peaks, and the ground is too solid for traditional earth internment. Likewise, being mostly above the tree line, there is not enough fuel for cremation.

Pit Burial—Pacific Northwest Haida

Before white contact, the indigenous people of the American northwest coast, particularly the Haida, simply cast their dead into a large open pit behind the village.

Their flesh was left to the animals. But if one was a chief, shaman, or warrior, things were quite different.

The body was crushed with clubs until it fit into a small wooden box about the size of a piece of modern luggage. It was then fitted atop a totem pole in front of the longhouse of the man's tribe where the various icons of the totem acted as guardians for the spirits' journey to the next world.

Written history left to us by the first missionaries to the area all speak of an unbelievable stench at most of these villages. Today, this practice is outlawed.

Viking Burial—Scandinavia

We have all seen images of a Viking funeral with the body laid out on the deck of a dragon ship, floating into the sunset while warriors fire flaming arrows to ignite the pyre.

Day of the Dead

The annual Mexican celebration, Día de Muertos (Day of the Dead), is a time when families gather to honor and remember deceased loved ones. It is believed that the souls of the dead return to visit the living families in homes, businesses and cemeteries.

Día de Muertos festivity takes place at the end of October and November 1st and 2nd each year in Mexico. This is a joyful festivity for families and the community. Music is played at home and at the cemeteries. Entire Mexican families construct traditional ofrendas (altars, offerings) that reflect a mixture of Catholicism and ancient Mexican/Aztec cultural practices.

Anything can be placed on the altar for the visiting souls, including traditional food, fresh flowers, pan de muerto (or bread for the dead), candles, copal incense (aromatic tree resin), fruits, cloths, photographs, favorite drinks of the deceased, sugar folk toys, religious images and clothing. Most importantly, a photograph of the departed soul is placed on the altar. Pan de muerto, bread for the dead, is sweet and baked in shapes of skulls and human figures.

The flower of the dead is called Cempasúchil (Náhuatl, or Aztec, name for marigold). While orange and yellow marigolds are the main flowers, magenta terciopelo (ruby coxcombs) and nube (baby's breath) are also traditionally displayed. Copal (tree resin) is used as incense and is a symbolic transformation of the physical to the supernatural, associated with the death of the soul returning to the ofrenda. The name of each departed is written on a sugar skull. These sugar skulls are eaten and the living come to associate pleasant sensations with the sadness of death. Candles and fresh marigold flowers are placed on the altar to light and guide the way of the souls to the altar. Paths are marked with flower petals showing the departed souls the way to the altar. Day of the Dead toys are also placed on the altar. Painted clay skeleton figures portray the dead resuming their normal activities such as playing. Pull toys, coffins and crank boxes are displayed for the dead to play with. Living with death in this way means that Mexicans learn to accept death as part of life.

"What Is the Meaning of the Day of the Dead," Dayofthedeadnyc.org.

While very dramatic, burning a ship is quite expensive, and not very practical.

What we do know is most Vikings, being a sea faring people, were interred in large graves dug in the shape of a ship and lined with rocks. The person's belongings and food were placed beside them. Men took their weapons to the next world, while women were laid to rest wearing their finest jewelry and accessories.

If the deceased was a nobleman or great warrior, his woman was passed from man to man in his tribe, who all made love to her (some would say raped) before strangling her, and placing her next to the body of her man. Thankfully this practice is now, for the most part, extinct.

Fire Burial—Bali

On the mostly Hindu Isle of Bali, fire is the vehicle to the next life. The body or Mayat is bathed and laid out on a table where food offerings are laid beside it for the journey.

Lanterns line the path to the person's hut to let people know he or she has passed, and act as a reminder of their life so they are not forgotten.

It is then interred in a mass grave with others from the same village who have passed on until it is deemed there are a sufficient number of bodies to hold a cremation.

The bodies are unearthed, cleaned, and stacked on an elaborate float, gloriously decorated by the entire village and adorned with flowers. The float is paraded through the village to the central square where it is consumed by flames, and marks the beginning of a massive feast to honor and remember the dead.

Spirit Offerings—Southeast Asia

Throughout most of Southeast Asia, people have been buried in the fields where they lived and worked. It is common to see large stone monuments in the middle of a pasture of cows or water buffalo.

The Vietnamese leave thick wads of counterfeit money under rocks on these monuments so the deceased can buy whatever they need on their way to the next life.

In Cambodia and Thailand, wooden "spirit houses" sit in front of almost every hut from the poorest to the most elaborate estate. These are places where food and drink are left periodically for the souls of departed relatives to refuel when necessary. The offerings of both countries also ask the spirits of the relatives to watch over the lands and the families left behind.

Predator Burial—Maasai Tribe

The Maasai of East Africa are hereditary nomads who believe in a deity known as Enkai, but this is not a single being or entity.

It is a term that encompasses the earth, sky, and all that dwells below. It is a difficult concept for western minds that are more used to traditional religious beliefs than those of so-called primitive cultures.

Actual burial is reserved for chiefs as a sign of respect, while the common people are simply left outdoors for predators to dispose of, since Maasai believe dead bodies are harmful to the earth. To them when you are dead, you are simply gone. There is no after life.

Skull Burial—Kiribati

On the tiny island of Kiribati the deceased is laid out in their house for no less than three days and as long as twelve, depending on their status in the community. Friends and relatives make a pudding from the root of a local plant as an offering.

Several months after internment the body is exhumed and the skull removed, oiled, polished, and offered tobacco and food. After the remainder of the body is re-interred, traditional islanders keep the skull on a shelf in their home and believe the native god Nakaa welcomes the dead person's spirit in the northern end of the islands.

Cave Burial—Hawaii

In the Hawaiian Islands, a traditional burial takes place in a cave where the body is bent into a fetal position with hands and feet tied to keep it that way, then covered with a tapa cloth made from the bark of a mulberry bush.

Sometimes the internal organs are removed and the cavity filled with salt to preserve it. The bones are considered sacred and believed to have diving power. Many caves in Hawaii still contain these skeletons, particularly along the coast of Maui.

Ocean Burial

Since most of our planet is covered with water, burial at sea has long been the accepted norm for mariners the world over.

By international law, the captain of any ship, regardless of size or nationality has the authority to conduct an official burial service at sea.

The traditional burial shroud is a burlap bag, being cheap and plentiful, and long in use to carry cargo. The deceased is sewn inside and is weighted with rocks or other heavy debris to keep it from floating.

If available, the flag of their nation covers the bag while a service is conducted on deck. The body is then slid from under the flag, and deposited in Davy Jones locker.

In olden days, the British navy mandated that the final stitch in the bag had to go through the deceased person's lip, just to make sure they really were dead. (If they were still alive, having a needle passed through their skin would revive them).

It is quite possible that sea burial has been the main form of burial across the earth since before recorded history.

The Final Frontier

Today, if one has enough money, you can be launched into space aboard a private commercial satellite and a capsule containing your ashes will be in permanent orbit around the earth.

Perhaps this is the ultimate burial ceremony, or maybe the beginning of a whole new era in which man continues to find new and innovative ways to invoke spirits and provide a safe passage to whatever awaits us at the end of this life.

The World's Cities Are Running Out of Space for the Dead

Ana Naomi de Sousa

Just as the world's population is growing, so is the need to find space to bury the dead. In the following viewpoint Ana Naomi de Sousa talks about many modern cities where burial space in cemeteries is expensive and scarce, and the need for new ways to handle the dead. She also addresses cities and countries where other methods, such as grave recycling, are being used to handle the same problem. Sousa is a documentary filmmaker and journalist.

As you read, consider the following questions:

1. Why are cemeteries overcrowded in cities? What factors created this situation?
2. What is grave recycling?
3. How has a lack of space affected burial as a business?

L ack of space and soaring costs are familiar problems for anyone who lives in a city. From London to New York to Hong Kong, many are crammed into micro-apartments that cost hundreds of pounds or dollars a month to rent, unsure when they will be able to afford a more permanent abode.

And it may be a similar story when they die, too.

Some 55 million people are reckoned to pass away each year (about 0.8% of the planet's total population—equivalent to

100% of England's). Yet urban planners and developers focus overwhelmingly on accommodating and making money from the living. Cemeteries and columbaria (burial vaults) dating back hundreds of years retain an iconic place in our towns and cities—but, partly as a result of their limited profitability, most have not been allowed to grow. Which means metropolises the world over are running out of room to house their dead.

The problem is most acute in cities that do not practise grave recycling. Countries such as Singapore, Germany and Belgium offer public graves for free—but only for the first 20 or so years. Thereafter, families can either pay to keep them (often on a rental basis) or the graves are recycled, with the most recent residents moved further into the ground or to another site, often a mass grave.

It is a system that has worked efficiently for cities all over the world, particularly in Europe. Yet in countries where grave reuse is not the cultural norm, attempts to begin reusing plots—in cities such as Durban, Sydney and London—have faced resistance and accusations that religious and cultural traditions are being violated.

"In the UK we are in an acute crisis, largely because of our burial law," says Dr. Julie Rugg of the University of York's Cemetery Research Group, referring to legislation introduced in the 19th century that banned exhumation. "We have cemeteries of over 100 acres in London, but the way we use the space is not sustainable."

As a result of a change in church legislation, a small number of graveyards, such as the City of London cemetery, have recently—and quietly—begun reusing some graves older than 75 years, but this will not be enough to solve the city's burial problem. London's cemeteries will be completely full within the next 20-30 years.

Even cities that do practise grave recycling can run into problems. In Norway, concerns about sanitation and the risk of soil contamination in the 1950s led to a policy stipulating that all bodies be wrapped in plastic before burial. Years later, it was found that the bodies were not decomposing quickly enough in the plastic to allow the graves to be reused. Cemeteries were filling up at an unprecedented rate. A solution—injecting the graves with a lime

---

A History of Gravestones

In earlier times when there were no cemeteries, people used to have burial plots near their family homes. These graves were usually marked with rough stones, rocks, or wood, apparently, as a way to keep the dead from rising. They were mostly marked with the deceased's name, age, and year of death. Gradually, churchyard burials evolved involving large, square-shaped tombstones prepared from slate (1650-1900) or sandstone (1650-1890). The inscriptions carved on slate used to be shallow yet readable.

Public cemeteries evolved in the 19th century. Eventually, people started giving importance to the gravestones, headstones, footstones, etc. as a means to memorialize the dead. Thus, they started engraving the headstones with a small epitaph or a few words about the deceased whether written by the individual himself or by someone else. Plus, they bore details like the date of birth and date of death of the departed loved one.

The Victorian era (1837-1901) greatly emphasized customs and practices associated with death. So, the period paved way for elaborate tombstones and headstones. The cemeteries appeared more like parks as they had such lavish and decorated gravestones. In addition, the gravestones also included sculptured designs, artwork and symbols such as:

- angels of death
- star of David
- the Dove
- Egyptian symbol Ankh

---

solution to speed up decomposition—was eventually discovered by a graveyard worker, who charged the Norwegian authorities $670 per plot.

With space running out, the business of death has become highly lucrative as the cost of dying rises all over the world. "Burial is becoming more and more of a niche product or market," says Dr. John Troyer of the University of Bath's Centre for Death and Society. "The burial issue is not just about economics—but there is a lot about capital, capitalism and commodification involved."

Ed Koch, the former mayor of New York—a city with almost no burial plots left—pre-purchased his grave in Manhattan five

- Eye of Horus
- weeping willow tree
- maple leaf
- flowers
- horseshoe
- sword
- broken column

These symbols denoted religious beliefs, social class, occupation, and several other aspects of the life of the deceased.

Unlike these, most tombstone symbols from the Colonial period reflected fear of afterlife as they believed that only a few people would be allowed in the Heaven after death and the rest would be categorized as sinners.

Interestingly, in the 18th century, there emerged a short-lived burial practice of covering the graves with iron cages (mortsafes).

This strange practice, though, died out by the end of the Victorian era. The most popular materials for gravestones during this era were marble (1780-1930), granite (1860-until date), iron, and wood.

Earlier, gravestones were used only by the middle and upper classes. However, after the emergence of the new Protestant theology, even lower classes started using grave markers for commemorating the life of a departed loved one.

"History of Gravestones," International Southern Cemetery Gravestones Association.

years before his death in 2013 for $20,000. He described it as "a good investment" due to the rising prices.

In Hong Kong, where a series of hastily created hillside cemeteries consumed the city's last available burial space back in the 1980s, those still able to find and purchase a private grave can pay $30,000 for the privilege. Alternatively, there is an average five-year wait for a small spot in a public columbarium, where thousands of urns of cremated ashes are stored.

In some London boroughs, meanwhile, those unable to pay for a burial (currently costing around £4,500, and rising) are buried in multiple layers beneath the ground, in the style of the Victorians.

But without long-term public solutions to the burial land crisis, local authorities may end up outsourcing the problem.

"The private sector is sniffing around, realising there's a public concern for space running out," says Rugg. "We are shifting away from notion that cemeteries are a social service, towards saying there's no reason at all why we shouldn't institute charges to make cemeteries pay."

In 1963, Jessica Mitford published *The American Way of Death*, a scathing criticism of the funeral industry, which she accused of pushing up the cost of dying. In the decades since, both the UK and US have seen a cultural shift from burial towards cremation, which now accounts for about 70% of funerals in Britain.

But cremation creates as many problems as it solves. In both countries, urns still tend to be buried in cemeteries, and although many permit families to bury more than one urn in a single grave site, these still take up significant space—indefinitely. Cremation also poses increased environmental problems: it is an energy-intensive process, and the burning of dental fillings currently contributes to 15% of the UK's mercury emissions. (One potential alternative, "resomation"—whereby the body is chemically reduced to ashes and non-toxic waste water—is currently only legal in a few US states, despite having been under discussion in the UK and some other European countries for years.)

While an increasing number of people opt for "green burials"—which tend to involve burials in meadow and woodland sites, in biodegradable shrouds or caskets made of anything from cardboard to banana leaf—others ponder the role cemeteries play in our cities, and what it would mean if we lost them altogether.

"I tend to think of cemeteries as being like schools and hospitals," says Rugg. "They are an emotional locus … Without them, a neighbourhood is bereft of a particular kind of community space. Where else would you get that in an urban landscape? They add an emotional intelligence to a city."

Rugg talks of a not-too-distant future where vast, private cemeteries on the outskirts of cities accommodate graves rented out for short-term occupancy, and burials look more and more like a sub-sector of today's property market. Location and long tenure could become the privilege of a wealthy urban elite, while those unable to meet the rates find their mortal remains separated from those of their families, or relocated to less desirable locations—for as long as someone can pay the rent.

In Japan, large companies such as Panasonic already purchase corporate areas within graveyards for some of their employees. In Kuala Lumpur and several Asian cities, where cremation is a strict cultural norm, the lack of space and the need for a site where families can pay respects to their deceased has led to the invention of giant, mechanised columbaria, where thousands of urns are stored in a vault and can be retrieved with an electronic card. One private company, Nirvana, boasts 12 such sites across Malaysia, Singapore and Indonesia, and has plans for more—yet still it is oversubscribed. New alternatives are urgently needed.

Amid the scramble to accommodate the urban dead, one Hong Kong-based design studio has developed a prototype for an off-shore columbarium island called "Floating Eternity," which could hold 370,000 urns at sea. A cemetery design competition in Oslo, meanwhile, gave special mention to one student's design for a cemetery skyscraper that would reach hundreds of metres into the sky and include spaces for coffins, urns, a crematorium and a computerised memorial wall.

"A lot of people don't appreciate how deep graves can be," says Rugg. "If you turn a cemetery upside down it looks like the middle of the city—like a skyscraper. In the UK, the common graves of the 19th century, for example, are very, very deep." In fact, vertical cemeteries already exist all over the world, with Brazil's Memorial Necrópole Ecumênica in Santos standing tallest of all, at 14 storeys. It is the inspiration behind similar projects now under consideration in the crowded cities of Bogotá and Mumbai.

With the boundary between our virtual and physical lives becoming ever-more blurred, technology is sure to play a greater role in death, too. In Canada, Calgary's new "green" cemeteries have proposed using GPS locations, and hand-held satellite units instead of headstones, to help visitors find graves. In Japan, the company I-Can Corp. offers descendants online visits to virtual graveyards, where they can pour virtual water or light a virtual incense stick, instead of travelling the long distance to visit a grave in person.

Hong Kong's government went a step further, creating a social-media network of virtual graves aimed at families who had been forced to cremate their relatives' ashes—because of lack of space in the city—and so no longer had a physical space at which to pay their respects.

Troyer, however, offers a word of caution about this shift towards virtual graves. "A lot of the companies talking about digital solutions talk about 'forever'—and that's very complicated with the internet, because the virtual material we create can easily disappear. The lowly gravestone has been a very successful human technology, and I suspect it will last ... I would go with granite."

All Cultures Have Death Rituals

Jonathan Jong

In the following viewpoint Jonathan Jong argues that nearly all of the world's cultures celebrate death rituals. Some leave bodies of the dead out in the open in nature, while others entomb bodies in comfortable conditions. Some cultures bury the dead immediately while others mummify the body and keep it around for months. The author contends that these rituals, while ostensibly to celebrate the life of the deceased, are actually for the benefit of the living. And that comfort we receive in a time of grief is what all these diverse cultures have in common. Jong is a research fellow at Coventry University. His work focuses on the psychology of religion.

As you read, consider the following questions:

1. From what biblical book is the phrase "ashes to ashes, dust to dust" taken?
2. According to the viewpoint what two cultures are known to hire professional mourners for funerals?
3. What is the reason we ritualize death according to psychologists as mentioned in the viewpoint?

A shes to ashes, dust to dust. Few liturgical phrases from the 1662 Book of Common Prayer are so familiar to so many, even those who have never darkened the doors of a church. This

"From Mummification to 'Sky Burials': Why We Need Death Rituals," by Jonathan Jong, The Conversation, June 13, 2016. https://theconversation.com/from-mummification-to-sky-burials-why-we-need-death-rituals-60386 Licensed under CC BY-ND 4.0 International.

part of the funeral service, taken from the book of Genesis, is also reflected in what priests say when they sign the cross in ash on people's foreheads during Ash Wednesday: "You are made from dust, and to dust you shall return."

Death is central to Christianity. After all, its main symbol—the crucifix—is an instrument of torture and execution. Death also takes pride of place in the two central sacraments of the church. Baptism signifies a drowning in which one participates in the death of Jesus, as well as his resurrection. This death and resurrection are also regularly recalled in the celebration of the Eucharist (holy communion). Christians also observe special days dedicated to death, such as Good Friday and the feasts of All Souls and All Saints. Indeed, most saints' days fall on the dates of their deaths, rather than the anniversaries of their births.

From an anthropological and psychological standpoint, Christianity's apparent obsession with death is neither surprising nor special; religious traditions all over the world and across time are similarly morbid. Virtually all cultures have some sort of death ritual—varying from the simple to the extremely elaborate, the sanitised to the macabre.

The earliest evidence for human religion comes from Upper Palaeolithic burial sites dating from 50,000 to 100,000 years ago. It is difficult to know what our hominid ancestors believed, but grave goods and other similar burial practices indicate at least rudimentary afterlife beliefs. Even now, among the most common forms of religious practice is the veneration of the dead, such as in ancestor worship and devotion to saints.

Mortuary rituals are ubiquitous across cultures, but exactly how death is dressed up can differ widely. Kalahari bushmen, for example, leave corpses where they lie, then immediately abandon the area en masse, not returning for many years. This onerous move is not necessary for the sanitary disposal of corpses. But then nor for that matter are the expensive lined and cushioned mahogany or walnut caskets often used in modern Western burials.

And while Western funerals are often stoic affairs, others, such as those in many Mediterranean and Asian cultures, involve professional mourners who are paid to wail loudly. Bodies are variously entombed, buried, cremated or even excarnated. The Zoroastrians used to place corpses atop specially constructed Towers of Silence for the scavenging birds. Tibetans still practice "sky burials," leaving the bodies of their loved ones exposed on hill tops.

Muslims, for example, bury the body as quickly as possible—ideally before the next sunset. In other groups, such as in traditional Torajan society in Indonesia, the funeral might only occur months or years after a person's biological death. In the meantime, the corpse is mummified to prevent putrefaction and remains at home. It is dressed up and spoken to as if it were still a person. Even after the funeral, every few years there is a *ma'nene'*, during which the corpse is exhumed and given new clothing before reburial.

The Psychology of Rituals

The ritualisation of death is both universal and universally varied. But why? And is there anything that ties together the human tendency to make much ado about death? Across many different religious traditions, the well rehearsed answer is that we do so for the good of the dead: we venerate them and offer sacrifices to them for their benefit, to ease their passage into the afterlife. The psychologist's answer, perhaps predictably, is that we ritualise death for our own sake, to quell our own sorrows and anxieties. Indeed, there is increasing evidence that rituals in general do serve to regulate our emotional reactions.

Experiments conducted at Harvard University, for example, showed that rituals—even simple rituals just invented by the researchers—reduce people's feelings of grief, including grief over the death of a loved one. These studies also revealed that rituals aid bereavement by increasing people's sense of control. That is, rituals help us to feel less helpless in the face of loss. This evidence also complements previous findings from studies that associate absence of mortuary rituals with prolonged grief.

Rituals may also serve to stave off our own anxieties concerning mortality. Certainly, studies have shown that people's behaviour becomes ritualised—more rigid and repetitive—when they are put in stressful situations, which researchers interpret as being a means of reducing anxiety. Furthermore, group rituals, particularly those involving synchronous behaviour, also foster a sense of social cohesion that can help us to feel more physically formidable: rituals bind us together, which helps us when we are feeling threatened.

Another interesting idea not yet properly tested, which has its roots in the work of Sigmund Freud, is that ritualising death helps us to deal with the feelings of guilt associated with disposing of a corpse. We need symbolic rites that help us to reconceptualise the dead bodies of loved ones, so that they cease to be people and become objects that we can therefore abandon.

In a sense, Torajan death rituals of keeping dead bodies around for years could not be more different from the Muslim or Christian traditions, where most corpses are cremated to be buried or strewn, never to be seen again. And yet, despite this wide diversity of practice, it seems our death rituals serve the same psychological functions: to make us feel less helpless in the face of our sorrow and terror.

Periodical and Internet Sources Bibliography

The following articles have been selected to supplement the diverse views presented in this chapter.

"An Outline of Different Cultural Beliefs at the Time of Death." Loddon Mallee Regional Aplliative Care Consortium, September 2011. http://lmrpcc.org.au/admin/wp-content/uploads/2011/07/ Customs-Beliefs-Death-Dying.pdf.

Vaughan Bell, "We All Grieve in Our Own Way." *The Guardian*, November 24, 2012. https://www.theguardian.com/science/2012/ nov/25/grief-mourning-psychology-customs.

Alixe Bovey, "Death and the Afterlife: How Dying Affected the Living." British Library, April 30, 2015. https://www.bl.uk/the-middle-ages/articles/death-and-the-afterlife-how-dying-affected-the-living.

"Chinese Funeral Traditions." Dostal Funeral Services. http://www. dostalfuneralservices.com/download/13525/ChineseFuneralTr. pdf.

"Day of the Dead Observances Reflect a Blending of Cultures." *Dallas News*, October 2012. https://www.dallasnews.com/ news/news/2012/10/19/day-of-the-dead-observances-reflect-a-blending-of-cultures.

Emily Gaudette, "What Is Day of the Dead? How to Celebrate Dia De Los Muertos Without Being Offensive." *Newsweek*, October 31, 2017. http://www.newsweek.com/day-dead-dia-de-los-muertos-sugar-skulls-696811.

Nicola Heath, "Funeral Customs Around the World." SBS, April 12, 2016. https://www.sbs.com.au/topics/life/culture/explainer/ funeral-customs-around-world.

Phyllis Palgi and Henry Abramovitch, "Death: A Cross-Cultural Perspective." *Annual Review of Anthropology*, Vol. 13 (1984), pp. 385-417. https://www.uio.no/studier/emner/sv/sai/ SOSANT2555/PALGI_A_Cross-Cultural_Perspecive_2155675. pdf.

Tom Rachman, "Meeting Death with Words." *The New Yorker*, January 25, 2016. https://www.newyorker.com/culture/cultural-comment/meeting-death-with-words.

Kate Torgovnick May, "Death Is Not the End: Fascinating Funeral Traditions from Around the Globe." Ideas.Ted.com, October 12, 2013. https://ideas.ted.com/11-fascinating-funeral-traditions-from-around-the-globe/.

Logan Ward, "Top 10 Things to Know About the Day of the Dead." *National Geographic*. https://www.nationalgeographic.com/travel/destinations/north-america/mexico/top-ten-day-of-dead-mexico/.

GLOBALVIEWPOINTS

CHAPTER 3

Inheritance and the Legalities of Death

In England the Rules of Wills and Inheritance Are Changing

Jill Papworth and Patrick Collinson

In the following viewpoint Jill Papworth and Patrick Collinson discuss England's laws concerning wills and inheritances, with a special focus on how laws are changing to accommodate new social relationship patterns, such as unmarried partners and adopted children. The authors list some of the upcoming changes and advise readers as to how to ensure that their estate goes where they want it to after their death. Papworth is a writer for Guardian Money. *Collinson is money editor of* The Guardian *and the newspaper's personal finance editor.*

As you read, consider the following questions:

1. How have laws concerning wills and inheritances been affected by changing relationship patterns?
2. Based on the context in which it is used, what might "intestate" mean?
3. How have property laws changed for adopted children?

The biggest overhaul of laws governing what happens to someone's money when they die without a will come into force on 1 October—and "common law" partners may be shocked

"Wills and Inheritance: How Changes to the Intestacy Rules Affect You," by Jill Papworth and Patrick Collinson, Guardian News and Media Limited, September 20, 2014. Reprinted by permission.

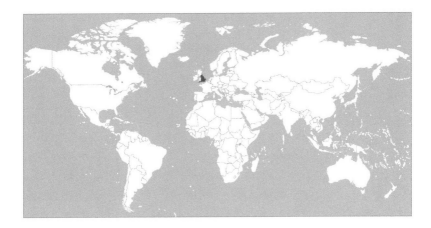

to discover they still have absolutely no protection, while the children of married partners may find they are in line for less than they thought.

If someone dies without a will, there is a set of intestacy rules that determine who gets what. The rule changes won't affect people who die with less than £250,000 in assets. But for those with more—and there's a growing number following the explosion in house prices—it could have a crucial impact on the people they leave behind.

Ahead of the changes, many lawyers were pressing for the partners in unmarried relationships to have rights over their deceased partner's estate if they had lived together for five years. Under current rules, co-habitees have no automatic right to receive a penny—regardless of how long they have lived together or even if they had children.

But the rules are staying the same: co-habitees get nothing. "One of the initial proposals that was not included in the agreed changes was to include co-habitees in the intestacy rules to reflect living circumstances in today's society," says James Antoniou, head of wills for the Co-operative Legal Services. "This would have seen a co-habitee treated like a spouse if they had been living with the deceased for at least five years up until death, or if they had children together and had been living together for at least two years up until death."

So it remains the case that the only way to ensure that part, or all, of your estate will go to your partner is to marry them, or make a will.

So what does change from 1 October?

The biggest change is for married couples and civil partnerships without children. Under the old rules, if a spouse died intestate and there were no children, then the first £450,000 of the estate, plus half of the rest, went to the surviving spouse. The other half was split between the deceased's blood relatives—which often meant the money went back to the parents.

For example, John is 52 and dies suddenly from a heart attack, leaving £750,000. Under the old rules, his wife Mary would have received £600,000—made up of the first £450,000 plus 50% of the rest, or £150,000. Let's say John's father has also died, but his mother is still alive. She would get the remaining £150,000.

But under the new rules, the chances of parents or more distant relatives getting a slice of the cash on death, have been swept away. From 1 October, the surviving spouse will receive the whole lot, and parents and long-lost aunties won't see a penny. In the example above, Mary will take the entire £750,000.

There are also some important changes to what happens if a married/civil-partnered couple have children. Under the old rules, the married partner took everything up to £250,000, with a complicated system for sharing out anything above that. Firstly, the children would receive half of the balance above £250,000 immediately (or held in trust to the age of 18). Secondly, the other half would also go to the children, but the surviving spouse would also have a "life interest" in the money while she remained alive. The life interest meant he or she could take income from the money, but not the capital.

But from 1 October, the life interest concept is abolished. The surviving married partner will take all of the first £250,000 and then be fully entitled to half of the remainder. All the children will get is half of anything above £250,000—and have to wait until 18 years old to get their hands on it.

Pecking Order

Rules of inheritance:

1. Children or their descendants
2. Parents
3. Brothers or sisters or their descendants
4. Half siblings or their descendants
5. Grandparents
6. Uncles and/or aunts or their descendants
7. Half uncles and/or aunts or their descendants
8. Whole estate passes to the crown

The new rules also eliminate a legal anomaly that affected adopted children. Under the old rules, if someone died leaving a child under the age of 18 who was subsequently adopted by someone else, there was a risk that the child would lose their inheritance from their natural parent. The new rules have closed that anomaly, so that there is no longer a risk of a child losing their inheritance if they are adopted after the death of their natural parent.

The definition of what is personal property or "chattels" also changes from 1 October. Under the old rules "chattels" had an archaic and arguably ambiguous definition, which included "carriages," "linen" and "scientific instruments." Under the new rules "chattels" are now defined as anything that is not monetary, business assets or "held as an investment." But this does not mean total clarity, Antoniou predicts.

"There will be disputes over what is meant by 'investment,'" he says. "People see investments as different things, and where there are collectable items of value in an estate, there may be a dispute over whether they pass to the new spouse as 'chattels,' or form part of the estate that the children from a previous marriage might inherit as an 'investment.'"

Powers of Attorney vs. Wills

Power of Attorney

In case you are seriously hurt in an accident or you become seriously ill, you need a power of attorney, otherwise you and your family may incur significant expense or lose control of your property, finances and even the ability to make decisions regarding your personal care if you become physically or mentally incapacitated.

There are basically two powers of attorney, one for personal care, (medical decisions) and one for property (i.e. land, bank accounts, pay bills, and investments).

With a power of attorney you can appoint one or more of the people you trust to look after you and your property instead of the Public Guardian and Trustee. This appointment can be made quickly and easily.

If you have not signed Powers of Attorney, imagine the surprise when your spouse, child, or someone close to you comes to visit you and is told the Public Guardian and Trustee is now deciding the level of comfort and care to be provided to you.

Wills

A will is a document prepared by you during your lifetime to take effect upon your death. It directs how the various assets and possessions you own will be disposed of when you die.

Then and Now—the Changes

Married/Civil Partner, no children

Before 1 October 2014

£450,000

- First £450,000 plus half of the rest goes to the spouse, remaining 50% to the blood relatives (parents, nieces, etc.).

- Example: Husband dies leaving £750,000. Wife receives £600,000. The husband's father has died, but his mother is still alive. She receives remaining £150,000.

Everyone should ensure that they have a valid legal will for at least two reasons: to state where your assets go and who would be the guardian of your children. If you do not have a will, matters are likely to be much more difficult and costly for your family. In addition, your assets may not be distributed in accordance with your wishes!

While a lawyer is not necessary to prepare a will, obtaining proper legal advice is strongly advised. Certain particular situations make it more imperative that a lawyer become involved, such as:

- Second Marriages—require legal advice because a prior will may be revoked
- Minor Children—parents/grandparents should make sure that children's assets are protected for them until they reach a certain age
- Parties who are under a disability
- Beneficiaries who are separated (both before and after a bequest)
- Large estates (including estates that have out of country properties or cottage properties)—should be given special attention because income tax consequences may come into play
- Children—you may wish to appoint a guardian but you may also wish to specify who has access to your children during the guardianship period

"What Is the Difference Between a Power of Attorney and a Will," Mann McCracken & Associates.

After 1 October
Whole estate

- Entire estate goes to spouse/civil partner.
- Example: Husband dies, total estate £750,000.
- Wife: Receives £750,000.
- Husband's mother: Receives nothing.

Married/Civil partner, with children
Before 1 October
£250,000

- First £250,000 goes to the spouse with half of the rest going to the children and the remainder going to them when the spouse dies. But while alive, the spouse keeps a "life interest" in half the money above £250,000 which lets them spend the income, but not touch the capital.

- Example Husband leaves £450,000. His wife receives £250,000. The remaining £200,000 goes to his sole child.

- But his wife keeps a "life interest" in this money.

After 1 October
£250,000

- First £250,000 plus half of the rest goes to the spouse. The remaining estate goes to the children. The "life interest" rule disappears.

Unmarried couple, no children
Before 1 October
£0

- Partner receives nothing.

- The entire estate goes to the deceased's blood relatives. First in line are parents, then siblings, then nieces and nephews.

- Example John dies, total estate £200,000. Partner of 20 years, Susan, receives nothing. John's parents have died, and his one brother, Jeff, has also passed away. Jeff had one child, Clare, who John barely spoke to. Clare receives all the money.

After 1 October
£0

- No change. Partner still receives nothing if there's no will. There is no such thing as "common law" protection, no matter how long the partners have lived together.

Unmarried couple, with children
Before 1 October
£0

- Partner receives nothing. The person is treated as if they are single.

- Example John has a son, Jack, from an earlier marriage, but is going out with Susan, who has a daughter, Jill, from her former partner. If John suddenly dies, Jack inherits the lot while Susan and Jill get nothing.

After 1 October
£0

- No change. The parents are treated as single people—with the estate going entirely to blood relatives, with children first in line.

In the United States the Estate Tax Is Increasingly Inefficient

Gary Robbins

Since the days of ancient Egypt, governments have often imposed death taxes on the estates of the deceased and their families. The author states that while estate taxes were once only a problem for the very rich, in today's world with a better economy, more people are finding themselves affected by them. He also presents an overview of the history of these kinds of taxes. Robbins is former Visiting Fellow in Tax Policy at The Heritage Foundation and president of Fiscal Associates.

As you read, consider the following questions:

1. Why have estate and death taxes become important to more than just extremely wealthy people?
2. What was one of the earliest known incidents of death taxes?
3. How did a 20th century drop in tariffs affect estate taxes?

Until recently, estate taxes (also known as death taxes) were the almost exclusive headache of the super rich, their tax attorneys, and their estate planners. But a strong economy, an ever-widening distribution of wealth—both good things—coupled with tax policy that has failed to keep up with economic growth have extended the reach of estate taxes well into middle-class America.

"Estate Taxes: An Historical Perspective," by Gary Robbins, The Heritage Foundation, January 16, 2004. Reprinted by permission.

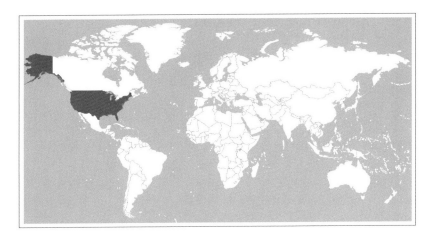

A Brief History of the Estate Tax

Estate taxes are not a new phenomenon; they date back almost three thousand years. As early as 700 BC, there appears to have been a 10 percent tax on the transfer of property at death in Egypt.[1] In the first century AD, Augustus Caesar imposed a tax on successions and legacies to all but close relatives.

Transfer taxes during the Middle Ages grew out of the fact that the sovereign or the state owned all assets. Although the king owned all real property in feudal England, he would grant its use to certain individuals during their lifetimes. When they died, the king would let the estate retain the property upon payment of an estate tax.

In the United States, the tradition of taxing assets at death began with the Stamp Act of 1797. While the first Stamp Act on tea helped precipitate the Revolutionary War, the second was far less dramatic. Revenues from requiring a federal stamp on wills in probate were used to pay off debts incurred during the undeclared naval war with France in 1794. Congress repealed the Stamp Act in 1802.

That set a pattern for the next hundred years or so in which estate taxes were used as a sporadic, and temporary, way to finance wars. When hostilities ceased, the tax was repealed.

To help finance the Civil War, the Tax Act of 1862 imposed a federal inheritance tax. As costs mounted, the Congress increased the inheritance tax rates and added a succession tax in 1864. When the need for added revenue subsided after the war, the inheritance tax was repealed in 1870.

In 1874, a taxpayer challenged the legality of the Civil War estate taxes, arguing they were direct taxes that, under the Constitution, must be apportioned among the states according to the census. The Supreme Court disagreed saying that direct taxes pertained to capitation taxes and taxes on land, houses, and other permanent real estate.[2]

Another legal decision bearing on, but not directly related to, estate taxes concerned the Income Tax Act of 1894, which included gifts and inheritances as income subject to tax. The Supreme Court struck down the whole bill because the tax was imposed on, among other things, real estate gains and, therefore, was considered a direct tax.[3] This decision is particularly notable because it set the stage for the Sixteenth Amendment that allows the federal government great latitude in the types of taxes it can collect.

The Modern Estate Tax Evolves: 1916 to 1975

In the early 20th century, worldwide conflict cut into trade tariffs—a mainstay of federal revenues—and Congress turned to another revenue source. The Revenue Act of 1916, which introduced the modern-day income tax, also contained an estate tax with many features of today's system. After an exemption of $50,000 (over $11 million in terms of today's wealth), tax rates started at 1 percent and climbed to 10 percent on estates over $5 million (over $1 billion in terms of today's wealth). Estate taxes were increased in 1917 as the US entered World War I.

However, this time the estate tax did not go away after the war ended. Despite sizable budget surpluses, Congress increased rates and introduced a gift tax in 1924. Like the estate tax, the gift tax is a levy on the transfer of property from one person to another. During the 1920s through the 1940s, estate taxes were used as another way to attempt to redistribute income. Tax rates of up to 77 percent on the largest estates were supposed to prevent wealth becoming increasingly concentrated in the hands of a few.

While the Internal Revenue Code of 1954 overhauled the federal income tax, it made a seemingly minor structural change to estate taxation. Specifically, it expanded the tax base to include most life insurance proceeds, which could substantially raise an estate's tax bill.

Reshaping Federal Transfer Taxes: 1976 to the Present

During the late 1960s and early 1970s loophole closing preoccupied tax reformers. These efforts culminated in a 1976 tax bill that overhauled estate taxation, giving us the system we still have today. Perhaps the biggest change was combining the previously separate exemptions for estate and gift taxes and transforming them into a single, unified estate and gift tax credit.

The 1981 tax bill brought some relief. The top rate went from 70 percent to 50 percent, and an increase in the unified credit took a lot of smaller estates—those under $600,000—off the tax rolls. But, after that, the search for revenue to close budget deficits led to more than a decade of bills that largely increased estate taxes.

In 1997, Congress provided some relief with the first increase in the unified credit since 1987. Gradual increases, which began in 1999, are slated to raise the unified credit to $1 million by 2006.

The Economic Growth and Tax Relief Reconciliation Act of 2001 was the first step toward totally eliminating the death tax. It provides for a scheduled phase-out of rates and an increase in the unified credit, finally repealing the tax for calendar year 2010. Unfortunately, the provisions sunset in 2011 and the estate tax reverts back to the 1997 law with a top rate of 55 percent and a unified credit of $1 million.

Estate Taxes and the Economy

The estate tax has a large dead-weight loss. Because the estate tax falls on assets, it reduces incentives to save and invest and, therefore, hampers growth. Along with income taxes, estate taxes help raise the tax rate on income from assets relative to income from working. This unequal treatment of income leads to an inefficient mix of capital and labor.

The size of the dead-weight loss depends on how much of a nation's assets are subject to the tax and the amount of distortion. The estate tax exemption determines the proportion of wealth covered and the rate structure determines the degree of the distortion.

A rough measure of the distortion is the ratio of marginal to average rates for those paying the tax. The average rate is a proxy for the amount of revenue raised, while the marginal rate is a proxy for the overall price distortion. Under a uniform tax, the ratio would be one and the amount of distortion would be minimized. The greater the difference between the marginal and average tax rates, however, the greater the distortion and, therefore, the larger the dead-weight loss.

Currently, the marginal estate tax rate is nearly three times higher than the average. Even though the estate tax rate structure is progressive, the high ratio is due mostly to the unified credit. In 1916, the statutory exemption was $50,000. Adjusting the exemption for the growth in wealth between 1916 and 2003 indicates that estates under $11 million (in today's wealth) would not be taxed. In 1931, the exemption was worth even more—$14.1 million (in today's wealth). However, since then the real value of the exemption has fallen dramatically. The low of about $356,000 was reached in 1976.

Tax bills in 1981 and 1997 provided modest increases in the exemption. However, the exemption of $675,000 in 2001 is still a far cry from its $11 million counterpart in 1916. This failure of the estate tax exemption to keep up with rising wealth is the main reason increasing numbers of average Americans face the prospect of having their heirs presented with an estate tax bill. A middle class family that owns a home and has IRAs, 401(k)s, or other retirement accounts could easily have assets exceeding $675,000 today or even $1 million five years from now.

While the eroding exemption has greatly expanded the estate tax base, both the lowest and highest tax rates also have gone up significantly since 1916. As a result, more of a taxable estate is taxed at the highest marginal rate. In 1916, only estates over $1 billion (in today's wealth) would have been taxed at the top rate of 10 percent. Contrast that with the top rate of 55 percent on estates of $3 million in place in 2001 (and possibly again in 2013).

The applicable rates are more compressed because of the unified credit. Under an exemption system, the estate would begin paying tax at the lowest statutory rate. Under the credit, however, the effective bottom rate is not the statutory 18 percent shown in the graph, but 39 percent. While effective tax rates under the 1997 law ranged from 39 percent to 55 percent, as the credit continued to erode in value, the lowest effective rate rose to 41 percent by 2002 and will appear again in 2011.

Effect on Family Business

The estate tax is particularly harmful to families that own businesses or farms. Even though the amount of the tax is based on asset value, the simple fact is that the tax must be paid out of income.

Let us look at two small business examples. Take a family-run store yielding a 10 percent return each year. Taxes reduce the return to 5 percent.[4] If the owner dies and his estate is subject to the 55 percent estate tax rate, how do the heirs pay the bill? They could send 55 percent of the store's inventory or other physical assets to Washington, except Treasury does not accept payment-in-kind, only cash. Devoting the entire 5 percent annual return, the heirs could pay off the estate tax in only 11 years, except Treasury wants the money now. The heirs could borrow from the bank at 9 percent (4.5 percent after tax) and pay off the loan in 50 years, but rather than run the store for 50 years for free, they probably would sell.

This example is not as outlandish as one might think. Consider the small farmer who owns land near an urban area. His farm would yield a 10 percent return only when it is valued as farmland. But tax law requires that the asset be valued at its "best use," lowering the pre-tax return to 5 percent (2.5% after tax). In this case, even the 50-year bank loan will not save the farm.

The lesson to be learned here is that all taxes are paid out of income. Even if the estate tax is a "rare" event, only one chance in a lifetime, its average impact is very large—large enough that for some the combined effects of income and estate taxes approach 100 percent.[5] The prospect is that as much as 55 percent of the principal of any investment will be taken in estate taxes on top of income taxes. In cases like these, the clear message is "don't invest, consume."

The Congress has tried to address the hardship circumstances for farmers and small business in general. But the remedy effectively has the government standing in for the bank. The final result is the same—heirs are left with a choice of owning a nonperforming asset for a number of years or simply selling. What is more, the IRS has taken these half measures as an excuse to raise appraised estate values, thereby reducing the tax relief.

The investment decision becomes even more complicated if there are ways to organize holdings to pass the income stream to heirs. Tax planning can significantly mitigate the effect of the estate tax. Because amounts involved tend to be large, estate planning richly rewards taxpayers who can anticipate that they might be subject to the tax. Those that do not plan or cannot anticipate are caught and pay the tax. This is simply unfair.

That is one reason why the largest estates do not pay the highest tax rates. Who does? Typically they are owners of small businesses, family farms, and savers who amass wealth during their lifetimes through hard work and thrift. Because wealth is often unexpected, these people may not be aware of, or take full advantage of, ways to reduce estate taxes. As a result, those who come late, or not at all, to estate planning end up paying most of the tax.

Conclusion

The estate tax is one of the most inefficient features of the current tax system. Its sheer complexity results in high compliance costs—as much as estate taxes raise by some estimates. High compliance costs along with distortions to economic activity warrant outright elimination of estate taxes before the sunset occurs.[6]

Failing repeal after 2010, the exemption should be raised significantly. Increasing the exemption to the range of $5 million to $10 million would restore eroded value and reduce the proportion of wealth subject to tax to be more in line with the 1920s and 1930s.

This would only partially address the impact of the tax, however. Under the unified credit structure, raising the exempt amount above $3 million would make the lowest marginal rate 55 percent, meaning the tax would be even less efficient than current law. While the amount of wealth subject to tax would be reduced, the rate structure would be harsher, increasing the ratio of marginal to average rates. The way to avoid this result is to convert the exemption from a credit to a deduction.

Another desirable change would be to expand the rate brackets and lower rates. As we have seen the current rate brackets have become compressed when compared to prior law. Expanding the brackets would reduce the marginal rate relative to the average and produce a more efficient system. Similarly, reducing estate tax rates would also help to improve the system. The best solution, however, would be to eliminate the estate and gift tax altogether before the sunset.

Notes

1. More on the history of estate taxes is available in John R. Luckey, "A History of Federal Estate, Gift and Generation-Skipping Taxes," Congressional Research Service, March 16, 1995, and Martha Britton Eller, "Federal Taxation of Wealth Transfers, 1992-1995," SOI Bulletin, Winter 1996-97.
2. Scholey v. Rew, 23 Wall. (90 U.S.) 331 (1874).
3. Pollock v. Farmers' Loan and Trust Company, 158 U.S. 429 (1895).

4. A tax rate of 50 percent might seem high, but we calculate the economy-wide, marginal tax rate on private business capital at roughly 67 percent.
5. The impact of a tax imposed on assets must be multiplied by one divided by the after-tax rate of return. Thus, the impact of the estate tax is magnified by 10 for an asset with an after-tax return of 10 percent and by 20 for an asset with a 5 percent return.
6. The 108th Congress has the chance to permanently repeal this burdensome and inefficient tax in the current session. The House already has voted to do so, and the Senate should not let this opportunity to build on the momentum of the 2001 tax cuts slip away.

Estate and Inheritance Taxes Are a Poor Source of Economic Revenue

Alan Cole

In the following viewpoint Alan Cole compares death and estate taxes around the world and presents an argument for these taxes being poor economic policy and something that should be phased out. The author argues this could ultimately boost the worldwide economy. Cole was an Economist with the Center for Federal Tax Policy at the Tax Foundation from 2013 to 2017. His research on federal taxes has been cited in Congress and in newspapers around the country.

As you read, consider the following questions:

1. Why does the author claim that estate and inheritance taxes are "poor economic policy"?
2. Why are many countries eliminating death and estate taxes?
3. Why might repealing estate and death taxes help the US economy grow?

The United States is one of many countries that levies taxes on estates or inheritances. This report compares this aspect of the US tax system to other countries around the world and examines recent worldwide trends in estate and inheritance taxes.

"Estate and Inheritance Taxes Around the World," by Alan Cole, Tax Foundation, March 17, 2015. Reprinted by permission.

Estate and inheritance taxes are broadly similar because both are generally triggered by death. Estate taxes are levied on the net value of property owned by a deceased person on the date of their death. In contrast, inheritance taxes are levied on the recipients of the property. Both of these taxes are generally paired with some kind of gift tax so that they cannot be avoided by simply transferring the property prior to death.

Estate and inheritance taxes are poor economic policy. They fall almost exclusively on the domestic capital stock—the accumulated wealth that makes America richer and more productive as a whole. Taxes levied on the capital stock restrict job growth and harm the economy. This study finds that repealing the US estate tax would lead to the creation of nearly 150,000 jobs and would eventually increase federal tax receipts by $8 billion per year.

Most countries that levy estate or inheritance taxes do so with lower top rates than the rate in the US. The US under current law has a high top rate and a large exemption. As a result, its estate tax, despite the high rate, raises very little revenue.

Many countries have recognized that estate and inheritance taxes are a poor source of revenue and eliminated these taxes altogether. Given low revenue collections, high compliance costs, and a narrow base, the US should seriously consider following suit.

The United States Has the Fourth Highest Estate or Inheritance Tax Rate in the OECD

A survey of top estate and inheritance tax rates among the Organization for Economic Cooperation and Development (OECD) countries shows that the US has a very high top marginal rate on estates by worldwide standards. At the margin, an estate passed to a lineal heir is currently taxed at a rate of forty cents on the dollar, putting it at fourth overall, tied with the United Kingdom.

The highest top estate tax rate to lineal heirs can be found in Japan, at 55 percent. South Korea (50 percent) and France (45 percent) also have rates higher than the US. At the low end, fifteen of the thirty-four countries in the OECD have no taxes on property passed to lineal heirs. The average estate tax rate across the OECD is 15 percent with a median tax rate of 7 percent.

The Eroding Tax Base Is an Increasingly Inefficient Source of Revenue

Many countries with estate or inheritance taxes have exemptions. This achieves two aims. First, exemptions are a simple way to make taxes more progressive. Second, these particular taxes have high compliance and enforcement costs. Assessing the value of people's assets is difficult, and it is not a worthwhile pursuit if those assets are not particularly valuable.

The US estate tax has an exemption of $5,430,000 in 2015. This is considerably larger than the exemptions in France ($105,945), Germany ($423,782), Japan ($247,297), and the UK ($488,280).[1] The US exemption has grown substantially in the last fifteen years.

The peculiar path of the exemption—including the year of full repeal—comes from the Economic Growth and Tax Relief Reconciliation Act of 2001, which was scheduled to sunset at the end of 2010. A subsequent bill, the Tax Relief, Unemployment Insurance Reauthorization, and Job Creation Act of 2010, reinstated the estate tax but with a higher exemption than before. Finally, the current law structure was put into place by the American Taxpayer Relief Act of 2012, also known as the "fiscal cliff" deal.

Exemptions tend to have a substantial impact on revenues. Revenues from the estate tax have declined precipitously as the exemption has increased, lowering the number of estates required to pay. A Tax Policy Center simulation from 2013 estimated that less than 4,000 estates would trigger an estate tax liability that year.[2] While a relatively small number of estates pay the tax each year, many more have to plan for the tax. Privately-owned businesses of all sizes spend money on this expensive endeavor.

In total, current revenues from the estate tax are barely half of what they were in real terms at the start of the millennium. The tax raised almost $38 billion (2015 dollars) in 2001, and it will raise only $20 billion in 2015, according to the most recent estimates from the Office of Management and Budget.[3] This is less than 1 percent of annual federal revenue.

As exemptions and tax planning strategies chip away at the tax and narrow its base, the tax becomes less and less worthwhile as a source of revenue.

Many Countries Have Eliminated Their Inheritance or Estate Taxes

As the United States maintains one of the highest estate taxes in the world, many countries are increasingly moving to eliminate this tax. As revenue dwindles, the fiscal benefits of the tax to the government are eventually outweighed by the administrative, political, and economic costs of levying a tax on a narrow base, and repeal becomes a more and more viable option.

Eleven countries and two tax jurisdictions have repealed their estate or inheritance taxes since the year 2000. The two tax jurisdictions to repeal were Macau and Hong Kong, which brought them in line with the rest of mainland China.

Also notable for eliminating their inheritance and estate taxes were Norway and Sweden, countries usually known for progressive politics. For example, the Social Democratic Workers' Party of Sweden repealed the tax in 2005. Their example reveals something important about estate tax repeal: interest can be independent of ideology. Even governments that like high revenues for robust social welfare spending find that estate or inheritance taxes are not an effective source. The experiences of these countries have been largely positive. In 2013, IKEA founder Ingvar Kamprad returned to his home country of Sweden after forty years of living abroad for tax reasons.[4]

Repealing the Estate Tax Would Grow the Economy

Repealing the estate tax in the United States would increase investment, add jobs, and expand the economy. The estate tax has a narrow base and a high rate, and it falls almost exclusively on the domestic capital stock. The capital stock (accumulated wealth) makes America more prosperous and productive as a whole, so taxes levied on the capital stock have unusually poor effects on economic growth.

Under the Tax Foundation Taxes and Growth Model, a simulated elimination of the estate tax results in approximately 150,000 additional jobs and 0.08 percent additional annual GDP growth in the decade after elimination. The static revenue loss of $20 billion per year would gradually be recouped through higher levels of wealth accumulation, and therefore, higher receipts from individual income taxes, payroll taxes, and corporate income taxes. In the long-run, the repeal would result in higher annual federal revenue of $8 billion due to the increased economic growth.[5]

In addition to the weak revenue numbers, the estate tax creates a cottage industry of tax planning, where skilled lawyers and accountants—people who could be more gainfully employed in the productive economy—instead devote energy to lowering the assessed value of estates. These losses, unseen and difficult to estimate, could be the greater concern.

Conclusion

Of all America's taxes, the estate tax is perhaps the most contentious.[6] On one hand, there is the compelling and deeply American ideal of equal opportunity. On the other, there is another ideal, no less compelling and no less American: that we ought to give our children better than we ourselves received.

These two ideas in civic culture are both seen as unqualified virtues. In truth, though, they are often in conflict with each other, no matter how noble each one seems in isolation. The debate over the estate tax is a manifestation of that conflict. This makes sense in the abstract.

However, in practice, the association between estate taxes and equality is not strong. The estate tax is ineffective at equalizing opportunity, just as it is ineffective at its other goals. Its low revenues speak to that ineffectiveness.

The estate tax is losing ground around the world, not because moral conundrums have been resolved, but rather because it fails at the basic characteristics of being a tax. Its rate is high, causing a substantial drag on growth. Its base is narrow, making it a poor revenue raiser. And lastly, its base is poorly-defined, creating additional economic losses from tax planning.

The ultimate purpose of tax collection is revenue generation. Due to the properties described above, the estate tax fails at effectively achieving that end. Eliminating it is the most serious option for reform.

Endnotes

1. Family Business Coalition data. These exemptions are, by statute, denominated in the native currencies of their respective countries. Their values in dollar terms change daily with foreign exchange rates, but by any reasonable measure all of these exemptions are substantially lower than the US exemption.
2. Benjamin Harris, Estate Taxes After ATRA, Tax Notes, February 25, 2013.
3. Office of Management and Budget, Table 2.5, Composition of Other Receipts, http://www.whitehouse.gov/omb/budget/Historicals.
4. Jens Hansegard, IKEA Founder Ingvar Kamprad to Move Back to Sweden, *Wall Street Journal* (June 27, 2013), http://www.wsj.com/articles/SB10001424127887324328204578571182799372930.
5. The Tax Foundation Taxes and Growth Model is a neoclassical production function of the US economy.
6. A Harris Interactive poll of US adults rated the estate tax as the least fair federal tax, with a score of 3.9 on a scale of one to five. See Tax Foundation, Poll: Tax Code Complex, Needs Reform; Federal Income Taxes "Too High" (Apr. 9, 2009), https://taxfoundation.org/article/poll-tax-code-complex-needs-reform-federal-incomes-taxes-too-high.

Death Can Result in Family Conflict Concerning an Estate

Mark Accettura

Sadly, the death of a family member can often create serious conflicts among the remaining family members as to inheritances, heirlooms, and who gets what. In the following viewpoint Mark Accettura presents recommendations for avoiding, minimizing, or dealing with existing conflicts in these situations. Accettura is an elder law attorney at Accettura & Hurwitz, Farmington Hills, Michigan, and author of Blood & Money: Why Families Fight Over Inheritance and What to Do About It *(Collinwood Press, 2012).*

As you read, consider the following questions:

1. How does good estate planning add to a healthy family legacy?
2. How do inheritance issues create conflict in families?
3. What are some things that can be done to minimize family conflict over inheritance?

You worked hard to build your nest egg. You saved, invested wisely and were careful to manage the myriad of risks that threatened your life's savings. Having invested so much time, effort and sacrifice into getting where you are, it only makes sense that

"18 Recommendations for Minimizing Inheritance Conflict," by Mark Accettura, American Association of Individual Investors, April 2012. Reprinted with permission from the American Association of Individual Investors 625 N. Michigan Ave., Suite 1900, Chicago, IL 60611,800-428-2244,www.aaii.com.

you would like to pass your life's work on to your loved ones with the least amount of tax and government interference.

There are well-established tools to ensure that your financial legacy reaches the intended recipients. Wills, revocable trusts, irrevocable trusts, family limited partnerships (and LLCs), private foundations, and an alphabet soup of strategies—like GRITs, GRATs, CRUTs, CRTs, and QPRTs, to name a few—make estate transition efficient and tax free for all but the truly wealthy, and therefore are an indispensable part of a secure financial plan.

Your Most Valuable Asset

But this article is not about current estate-planning strategies. Although an important subject, and one that occupies the estate planning community and the clients we serve, I want to talk about your most valuable and enduring asset, the asset that for better or worse survives you and impacts generations to come: family.

Family is truly the gift that keeps on giving. The family dynamic that you had a hand in creating will survive you, impacting your children and grandchildren. Although many of the events that went into forming your family as it now exists have already occurred, your family is not set in stone. How you live your life from this point forward and how you structure your estate at death are new opportunities to reinforce the healthy aspects of your family, correct past wrongs, and leave a lasting legacy of fairness, compassion and love.

Family survives long after an inheritance is either spent or is tucked away in the accounts of our beneficiaries. Despite our greatest efforts, wealth comes and goes. Even great wealth is often gone in a generation or two. History is replete with stories of successful entrepreneurs who amassed fortunes only to have them wasted within one or two generations after their death. The aphorism "shirt sleeves to shirt sleeves in three generations" describes this phenomenon and is said to derive from an old Lancashire (England) proverb "there's nobbut three generations atween a clog and clog," believed to have been imported to America by Andrew Carnegie. The transience of wealth has been lamented by many other cultures. The Italians, for example, in their classic lyrical style have an old expression: "Dalle stalle alle stelle alle stalle" ("from stalls to stars to stalls").

In addition to the transmission of wealth, our estate plan communicates many things to those we leave behind. We say who is remembered, who is loved, who is important, who we trust and who we trust to be in charge. It carries additional weight, because it is our final statement. Unlike fights or misunderstandings during life, we cannot take back or fix the insensitivities, oversights or hurtful provisions of our estate plan. The greatest slight is to not plan at all. By failing to plan, we communicate our apathy and the message that our loved ones were not worthy of being remembered. With so much at stake, we owe the process as much attention and thought as we can muster.

Anticipating and Avoiding Conflict

It is especially important to anticipate conflict. Inheritance conflict is often the final straw for challenged families, with members vowing to never speak to one another again. Special circumstances require special planning. If you have re-married, you must balance the financial and emotional needs of your spouse with those of your natural children. If your children don't get along, then you must choose fiduciaries carefully. Other unique factors require special attention, like a family business, a family cottage, or a handicapped or addicted child.

Ideally, as the parent, you should lead in the prevention effort. You are in the best position to create family peace and minimize future fighting. Use your position, perhaps as you never have, to build bridges and mend fences. You may not ultimately be able to undo the old hurts that brought the family to its current state, but you must never stop trying. You can best lead by having your estate affairs in order. Similar to succession planning in business, you need a transition plan and a transition team to implement your vision. Now is the time to take stock of your family portfolio. As the family CEO, you can implement a plan and secure the future course for your family and your assets.

The stepparent-stepchild relationship is particularly fraught with problems, as both vie for the love and affection of the natural parent. Children have difficulty understanding that their natural parent is, or was, a person with real needs that the stepparent fulfills or at one time fulfilled. Children must also understand that the stepparent has legitimate concerns about his or her economic well-being after the death of their spouse. Stepparents, in turn, must understand that children see their parent's inheritance as the final statement of love and that the stepparent is perceived as interfering with that connection. Finally, the natural parent in a second marriage must be sensitive to the personal dynamic between his children and the new spouse and take every step possible to keep the peace between both camps during life and after death.

Actions That Can Reduce Conflict

There is no single silver bullet that will prevent inheritance disputes. Instead, prevention requires a multi-faceted approach that combines psychology, good lawyering, a lot of self-awareness and a good dose of common sense. The following 18 recommendations are aimed at minimizing inheritance conflict:

1. Address Personal Property Separately

Leave a separate list of cherished personal property with instructions as to who should inherit each item. Personal property is often a source of conflict among family members.

Most states admit a separate personal property list (sometimes called a Personal Property Memorandum) as part of the will. A separate list can be handwritten or typed but must be signed and dated.

The list should be of sufficient detail to effectively describe each item being gifted.

2. Update Estate Plan Regularly

Make estate planning changes when there has been a change of circumstances, especially after a divorce.

Although most states' matrimonial laws nullify beneficiary designations and will provisions that favor former spouses, it is unclear whether a former spouse continues to be empowered under medical or financial powers of attorney. To avoid unwanted and bizarre results, former spouses should be immediately disinherited and stripped of all powers.

Additionally, estate planning should be reviewed after other life changes, like the death or divorce of a child or the illness, addiction or incapacitation of any beneficiary.

3. Hold an Open Discussion on Special Assets

There are situations where family input is advisable. Issues like care for a handicapped child, succession of a family business, or continued enjoyment of a vacation home require parents and children to be on the same page.

4. Consider a Prenuptial Agreement

Second marriages are one of the most significant indicators of inheritance conflict. A prenuptial or a post-nuptial agreement will minimize conflict at death by clearly stating the relative entitlements of spouses and other beneficiaries, such as children not of the marriage.

5. Clearly Identify Gifts and Loans

Parents often help adult children who are experiencing financial distress. It is the parent's prerogative to structure such advances as either loans or gifts. Unpaid loans from mom and dad can be a source of conflict, activating jealousies about who got more. Parents should resolve uncertainty regarding lifetime advances by addressing them in their estate plan.

6. Properly Fund Trusts

All assets should be funded or appropriately re-titled into a trust to avoid probate and confusion as to the testator's intent. For example, if the will or trust leaves equally among the testator's children, all life insurance policies and annuities should name the trust as beneficiary.

If for tax or other purposes it is appropriate to name beneficiaries directly, include a statement in the trust that all beneficiaries are to receive an equal share, taking into consideration assets that pass outside the trust.

7. Avoid Joint Ownership

Joint ownership (i.e., placing a child's name as a joint owner of a parent's asset) is an inefficient method of passing assets at death and can produce unintended results. Adding a beneficiary as an owner of assets like real estate confers significant and sometimes irrevocable lifetime rights, which expose the donor to the co-owner's liabilities and limits the donor's ability to change his or her mind in the future. The most efficient and predictable plan is to fund all assets into a trust.

8. Pre-Arrange Funeral Details

Making funeral arrangements and choosing the form of interment in advance can avoid conflict and the strong emotions that such decisions sometimes elicit. For example, re-married widows and widowers should determine in advance who is to be buried with whom. Pre-planned and detailed written funeral instructions avoid controversy and angst.

9. Name Spouse as Primary Fiduciary

Absent special circumstances, one's spouse in a first marriage should be named as primary and sole fiduciary. As recently as the 1970s, well-heeled husbands, even in first marriages, commonly named bank and trust companies as trustee of trusts established for their wife and children. Today, such arrangements would

Dealing with Conflict

Is there a correct way to handle conflict? What are the effects of poor conflict management? Conflict resolution is only a five-step process:

Step 1: Identify the source of the conflict. The more information you have about the cause of the conflict, the more easily you can help to resolve it. To get the information you need, use a series of questions to identify the cause, like, "When did you feel upset?" "Do you see a relationship between that and this incident?" "How did this incident begin?"

As a manager or supervisor, you need to give both parties the chance to share their side of the story. It will give you a better understanding of the situation, as well as demonstrate your impartiality.

Step 2: Look beyond the incident. Often, it is not the situation but the perspective on the situation that causes anger to fester and ultimately leads to a shouting match or other visible—and disruptive—evidence of a conflict.

The source of the conflict might be a minor problem that occurred months before, but the level of stress has grown to the point where the two parties have begun attacking each other personally instead of addressing the real problem.

Step 3: Request solutions. After getting each party's viewpoint on the conflict, the next step is to get each to identify how the situation could be changed. Again, question the parties to solicit their ideas: "How can you make things better between you?"

Just listen. You want to get the disputants to stop fighting and start cooperating, and that means steering the discussion away from finger pointing and toward ways of resolving the conflict.

Step 4: Identify solutions both disputants can support. You are listening for the most acceptable course of action. Point out the merits of various ideas, not only from each other's perspective, but in terms of the benefits to the organization.

Step 5: Agreement. The mediator needs to get the two parties to shake hands and agree to one of the alternatives identified in Step 4. Some mediators go as far as to write up a contract in which actions and time frames are specified.

This mediation process works between groups as well as individuals.

"The Five Steps to Conflict Resolution," American Management Association.

be unacceptable to most wives, as women have become full participants in the family economic unit.

In second marriages where there are children not of the marriage, each spouse should consider establishing his or her own separate revocable trust. While each spouse may act as the other's fiduciary, it may be preferable to appoint a neutral third party or professional (corporate) trustee to mediate the disparate interests of the surviving spouse and natural children. It is not advisable to name a spouse as co-fiduciary with children not of the marriage. Stepparents and stepchildren are natural competitors and in most cases should not be forced to work together.

10. Make Logically Defensible Choices

Determining who is "in charge" is an emotionally loaded issue. It is perceived as the testator's statement as to who is the most competent and trustworthy. Such decisions are reminiscent of the day when mom went to the store and put one of the children, usually the oldest, in charge. Mom hadn't left the driveway before younger children would protest: "You're not the boss of me," or more prophetically, "Who died and left you in charge?"

Appointing fiduciaries can be seen as an act of favoritism and should be thoughtfully considered. Naturally you want the best person for the job to ensure that your wishes are properly carried out. However, parents must still be sensitive to their children's emotional reactions.

Children can rationalize an older sibling being appointed simply on the basis of seniority. They can also accept the naming of in-towners over out-of-towners on the basis of convenience and geographic desirability. Children, however, cannot accept appointments that disturb the traditional family hierarchy and pecking order.

Where children are equally situated, appoint them as co-fiduciaries. Don't leave anybody out; name a younger or less-able child as successor to a successor if for no other reason than to show that you remembered them.

11. Be Aware of Long-Established Sibling Roles
In addition to age, name children on the basis of traditional family leadership roles. It is an insult in the order of disinheritance to take a leadership role away from a deserving child who has traditionally held that role and served it well.

12. Appoint a Committee
Naming a committee of fiduciaries has a number of benefits: Two heads are better than one; a committee keeps each member honest; communication with non-fiduciary beneficiaries is facilitated by having more than one spokesperson; and multiple fiduciaries can share the work load and minimize burnout and resentment.

Misunderstandings can quickly escalate when a single overburdened fiduciary fails to respond to beneficiary inquiries in a timely manner. In turn, a single fiduciary may resent repeated inquiries from what they perceive as greedy or overly-eager beneficiaries. The failure of an overburdened fiduciary to respond to inquiries in a timely manner raises suspicions that the fiduciary is trying to hide something.

A committee solves many of these problems and should be considered, as long as all of the members of the committee get along.

13. Recognize Primary Obligation When in First Marriage
Except where extenuating circumstances dictate, in first marriages one's surviving spouse should be named primary and sole beneficiary. A testator's first obligation is to his or her surviving spouse. As children can no longer be expected to care for ill or aging parents, spouses must leave each other in the best possible position to provide for their own needs. The risk that children will be disinherited is minimal, as they are the logical beneficiary of both spouses.

14. Balance the Needs of Second Spouses and Children
Care should be taken to accommodate the financial and emotional needs of both the surviving spouse and children. Consider an

outright transfer to natural children at the death of the first spouse of an amount that will not jeopardize the well-being of the surviving spouse.

Parents who completely withhold all distributions to their children until after the death of a stepparent create a potential deathwatch. There is no impatience like that of a stepchild waiting for their stepparent to die in order that they may receive what they believe to be rightfully theirs.

15. Leave to Children Equally and Disinherit Only as a Matter of Last Resort

Treat children equally. An unequal allocation is a blatant and unforgivable showing of favoritism that will re-activate old sibling rivalries and hurt feelings.

Children have unequal needs growing up. Some will naturally receive more based on special skills (travel sports, private schools, piano lessons), or special needs (braces, glasses, special shoes, or furlough from physical labor). However, the past is the past; don't be tempted to leave unequally at death to account for early inequities.

Don't penalize successful children by leaving more to their needy siblings, or conversely, reward successful children because they are favored. Exceptions to this general rule are the truly handicapped and those who would use their inheritance to further an unhealthy lifestyle of addiction or sloth.

Finally, be certain before you disinherit, as it leaves a lasting legacy of hurt and rejection.

16. Make Lifetime Gifts

Attempt to accommodate special needs through lifetime gifts. Lifetime gifts, like a dowry for a daughter or a stake for a son, have been used throughout history to accomplish inheritance objectives.

Be aware, however, that children have extremely sensitive antennae for detecting favoritism and are likely to become aware of such gifts.

17. *Transition Family Business*

A family business should pass to those family members who have been active in the business and who are instrumental to its future success. The fragile nature of businesses requires that there be a smooth transition from one generation to the next.

A seamless transition requires the gradual passing of the torch while parents are alive. Parents should groom their successors by gradually transferring responsibility and authority to their successors over time.

Non-business assets can be used to equalize the share for children not active in the business. Life insurance can be used to augment the value of the estate to ensure that sufficient assets are available to achieve an equal distribution to all children.

18. *Keep Estate Planning Content Private*

Clients often ask whether they should give a copy of their estate plan to their children. With the exception of health care powers of attorney (living wills), the answer for most families is "no."

As in the movie *Back to the Future*, you don't want knowledge of the future to affect the course of history. As author, you reserve the right to change the ending of your personal history. Giving documents during life creates the expectation that no changes will be made. Later changes will be viewed as taking away something previously given. We don't know the future; keep open the possibility that things may change.

Conclusion

Many of the problems of inheritance are themselves inherited. They are both genetic and acquired, but they are not inevitable. Inheritance disputes can be explained and predicted and are to a large degree preventable. By carefully and thoughtfully planning your estate, you can protect your most important legacy.

Wills Must Be Very Specific

HG.org

In addition to the distribution of an estate to family after a death, many people want to plan for certain items to go to non-family members after they die. In the following viewpoint authors from HG.org provide suggestions as to how best to make sure that items go where the deceased wants them to go. HG.org is an online source that makes legal information available to those in the law profession, businesses, and average consumers.

As you read, consider the following questions:

1. What is the biggest obstacle most people face when planning their estates?
2. Why are certain items and situations more likely to cause problems in settling estates?
3. Why might it be better to give possession to family and friends while you are still alive? Could this also cause problems?

Estate planning is not just about distributing your things after you are dead, it is about the relationships you have established in your life. While the law may dictate certain expedient ways that property should be distributed in the absence of other instructions, there are mechanisms that allow you to ensure that family and friends receive things from your estate that may have sentimental value. So, what do you think would be better? Ensuring that items

"Leaving Your Things to Friends After Your Death," HG.org. Reprinted by permission.

with special value pass to the people most likely to enjoy those memories, or just letting the whole lot get distributed to your family based on generic inheritance laws?

The biggest hurdle most people have to overcome when it comes to estate planning is their own reluctance to consider their mortality. You can leave items to people in your will or via a living trust, or you can give them away while you are still alive, but whatever you do you must make the plans now while you are alive and well. And, when it comes to leaving things to your friends (instead of your family) there is a good reason for that.

Inheritance laws do not recognize automatic distributions of your assets to anyone other than your direct and immediate family. The law will ensure that your spouse and children are provided for first, followed by parents, grandkids, and increasingly distant relatives if none of those other people exist. Even if you have zero living relatives, your belongings will not go to your friends; they will go to the government. So, if you want someone other than your family or the government to take anything from your estate after death, you have to make that wish known now.

There is another problem, though. If you think your family might fight the transfer of your property to friends, they may have a legal right to do so. If you intend to give something to a friend (or to keep something from going to your family) you may have to do it while you are still alive. While a gift given during your life while you are sane and able to make your own decisions will not generally be subject to challenge, any gifts you try to make after death, which would require the legal system to execute your plans will potentially be subject to challenge. So, it might be in everyone's best interest to give your things to your friends before you die.

Of course, not everyone knows they are near the end of their days with the time to give gifts of their belongings to friends. In those cases, you will need to create testamentary documents describing how you want your things to be distributed, and the distributions must not otherwise contradict the law. You should select someone to act as your executor or personal representative who will be likely to see your plans carried out as you wished and willing to fight on your behalf if family members object.

If you want to ensure that certain items go to certain people, your will needs to be very specific. In many states, you can make a separate list of items with information about and who you want to inherit them, then refer to that list in your will. You will not be able to distribute money or other intangible properties in this fashion, but actual possessions with sentimental value can go to whom you deem most appropriate.

Certain items are more likely to run into legal battles than others. For example, if you are married and have kids, leaving the house to your mistress is likely going to be a nonstarter for obvious public policy reasons. On the other hand, if you have a commemorative plaque that you earned with a long time work colleague, gifting that to someone in your will is less likely to trigger a significant dispute.

Unfortunately, laws pertaining to estate planning and inheritance rights vary widely between jurisdictions. Thus, for the best advice on how to plan your estate and make gifts of your belongings to the people you want to have them, you should contact an attorney in your area.

Periodical and Internet Sources Bibliography

The following articles have been selected to supplement the diverse views presented in this chapter.

Carol Bradley Bursack, "Siblings Who Care More About the Inheritance Than Parents' Care." Agingcare.com. https://www.agingcare.com/articles/sibling-who-only-care-about-inheritance-133713.htm.

Everplans, "8 Signs Your Family Will Fight Over Your Estate." Everplans. https://www.everplans.com/articles/8-signs-your-family-will-fight-over-your-estate.

Jay Folberg, "Mediating Family Property and Estate Conflicts: Keeping the Peace and Preserving Family Wealth." Mediate.com, 2009. https://www.mediate.com/articles/mediating_family_property.cfm.

Tim Grant, "Inheritance Conflicts Pit Relatives Against One Another." *Pittsburgh Post-Gazette*, July 3, 2014. http://www.post-gazette.com/business/2014/07/04/Inheritance-conflicts-pit-relatives-again-one-another/stories/201407020013.

"Inheritance Law and Your Rights." FindLaw. https://estate.findlaw.com/wills/inheritance-law-and-your-rights.html.

Darla Mercado, "Say Hello to the No. 1 Threat to Your $11 Million Inheritance." CNBC, April 11, 2018. https://www.cnbc.com/2018/04/11/family-conflicts-are-the-top-inheritance-threat.html.

Ilze Neethling, "The Psychology Behind Inheritance Conflicts: Wills Are Lit Fuses for Unfulfilled Emotional Needs and Family Break-Downs." Goodpsychology.net, November 23, 2013. https://www.goodpsychology.net/blog/the-psychology-behind-inheritance-conflicts-wills-arelightened-fuses-for-unfulfilled-emotional-needs-and-family-break-downs.

Mary W. Quigley, "How to Avoid Inheritance Fights Among Your Adult Kids." AARP, January 17, 2017. https://www.aarp.org/ home-family/friends-family/info-2017/avoid-inheritance-fights-mq.html.

Mary Randolph, "Common Terms in Wills and Trusts." Nolo. https:// www.nolo.com/legal-encyclopedia/common-terms-wills-trusts. html.

Kerri Anne Renzulli, "Half of Americans Don't Have a Will. Here's How to Fix That for Your Family." *Time*, November 30, 2016. http://time.com/money/4581727/estate-planning-inheritance-leave-money-will/.

Paul Sullivan, "When a Will Divides an Estate, and Also Divides a Family." *New York Times*, June 20, 2014. https://www.nytimes. com/2014/06/21/your-money/unequal-inheritances-may-ignite-family-squabbles.html.

GLOBAL VIEWPOINTS

The Legacies That Linger After Death

No One Wants Their Parents' Prized Possessions

Richard Eisenberg

In the following viewpoint Richard Eisenberg sets up a common scenario of children disposing of a parent's belongings after their death. He goes on to present examples of how many family objects and household goods do not actually have a great deal of value in themselves and may be difficult to dispose of. He gives clear advice as to how to deal with these objects and with cleaning out a household. Eisenberg is the Senior Web Editor of the Money & Security and Work & Purpose channels of Next Avenue and Managing Editor for the site. He is the author of How to Avoid a Mid-Life Financial Crisis *and has been a personal finance editor at* Money, Yahoo, Good Housekeeping, *and* CBS MoneyWatch.

As you read, consider the following questions:

1. Why don't young couples not usually want their parents and grandparents heirlooms?
2. What does the author mean when he calls today's young people the "Target and Ikea generation"?
3. Why is time—either having a lot of it, or very little of it—so important in disposing of possessions?

"Column: Need to unload family heirlooms? Prepare for disappointment" by Richard Eisenberg, Next Avenue, February 9, 2017.This article originated from Richard Eisenberg on Next Avenue (http://www.nextavenue.org)

A fter my father died at 94 in September, leaving my sister and me to empty his one-bedroom, independent-living New Jersey apartment, we learned the hard truth that others in their 50s and 60s need to know: Nobody wants the prized possessions of your parents—not even you or your kids.

Admittedly, that's an exaggeration. But it's not far off, due to changing tastes and homes. I'll explain why and what you can do as a result, shortly.

The Stuff of Nightmares

So please forgive the morbidity, but if you're lucky enough to still have one or more parents or stepparents alive, it would be wise to start figuring out what you'll do with their furniture, china, crystal, flatware, jewelry, artwork and tchotchkes when the mournful time comes. (I wish I had. My sister and I, forced to act quickly to avoid owing an extra months' rent on our dad's apartment, hired a hauler to cart away nearly everything we didn't want or wouldn't be donating, some of which he said he'd give to charity.)

Many boomers and Gen X'ers charged with disposing the family heirlooms, it seems, are unprepared for the reality and unwilling to face it.

"It's the biggest challenge our members have and it's getting worse," says Mary Kay Buysse, executive director of the National Association of Senior Move Managers.

"At least a half dozen times a year, families come to me and say: 'What do we do with all this stuff?'" says financial adviser Holly Kylen of Kylen Financials in Lititz, Pennslyvania. The answer: lots of luck.

Heirloom Today, Foregone Tomorrow

Dining room tables and chairs, end tables and armoires ("brown" pieces) have become furniture non grata. Antiques are antiquated. "Old mahogany stuff from my great aunt's house is basically worthless," says Chris Fultz, co-owner of Nova Liquidation, in Luray, Virginia.

How to Keep Heirlooms

When an aging loved one passes away, family members often feel compelled to split up some of their cherished belongings so they remain within the family, like old photographs, clothing, jewelry, or even furniture. However, how can you ensure they'll stay safe and preserved through the years for future generations?

You can ask yourself a few questions as you decide what you really should keep: Am I keeping this purely because it reminds me of someone, or because someone asked me to keep it? Do I have room to store this safely? Do I know the story behind this family heirloom?

If you do decide to part ways with any family heirlooms, you should first ask other family members if they would like the item; perhaps someone else would appreciate it and get more use out of it.

However, if you're keeping the items, knowing the proper way to store them is the first step in preserving these special pieces for future generations to enjoy. Here are a few tips for storing family heirlooms:

- Paper documents: Documents like birth certificates should be protected from moisture, heat and light. Don't fold or staple them, and keep them inside an envelope made of Mylar or acid-free paper. Place them flat in a file box, never upright.

- Clothing or fabrics: Fabric is also sensitive to moisture and light, and should be stored in a special preservation box containing tissue, muslin stuffing, moth balls or cedar chips.

- Photographs: Direct sunlight can cause the most harm to photographs, whether they are old or not. Photos should be framed with glass that offers UV protection if you're keeping them out on display. If you're storing photos, place them flat in sturdy boxes with a layer of acid-free tissue between them. Avoid storing photos in areas where temperature and humidity changes can wreak havoc on them.

- Jewelry: Keep jewelry in a velvet or satin-lined box. Silver jewelry should be wrapped in tissue paper or kept in a cloth bag to reduce tarnishing.

"Preserving and Storing Family Heirlooms," Self Storage Specialists, November 30, 2015.

On PBS's *Antiques Roadshow*, prices for certain types of period furniture have dropped so much that some episode reruns note current, lower estimated appraisals.

And if you're thinking your grown children will gladly accept your parents' items, if only for sentimental reasons, you're likely in for an unpleasant surprise.

"Young couples starting out don't want the same things people used to have," says Susan Devaney, president of National Association of Senior Move Managers and owner of The Mavins Group, a senior move manager in Westfield, New Jersey. "They're not picking out formal china patterns anymore. I have three sons. They don't want anything of mine. I totally get it."

The IKEA Generation

Buysse agrees. "This is an IKEA and Target generation. They live minimally, much more so than the boomers. They don't have the emotional connection to things that earlier generations did," she notes. "And they're more mobile. So they don't want a lot of heavy stuff dragging down a move across country for a new opportunity."

And you can pretty much forget about interesting your grown kids in the books that lined their grandparents' shelves for decades. If you're lucky, you might find buyers for some books by throwing a garage sale, or you could offer to donate them to your public library—if the books are in good condition.

Most antiques dealers (if you can even find one!) and auction houses have little appetite for your parents' stuff either. That's because their customers generally aren't interested. Carol Eppel, an antique dealer and director of the Minnesota Antiques Dealers Association in Stillwater, Minnesota, says her customers are far more intrigued by Fisher Price toy people and Arby's glasses with cartoon figures than sideboards and credenzas.

Even charities like Salvation Army and Goodwill frequently reject donations of home furnishings, I can sadly say from personal experience.

Midcentury, Yes; Depression-Era, No

A few kinds of home furnishings and possessions can still attract interest from buyers and collectors though. For instance, Midcentury Modern furniture—think Eames chairs and Knoll tables—is pretty trendy. And "very high-end pieces of furniture, good jewelry, good artwork and good Oriental rugs—I can generally help find a buyer for those," says Eppel.

"The problem most of us have," Eppel adds, "is our parents bought things that were mass-produced. They don't hold value and are so out of style. I don't think you'll ever find a good place to liquidate them."

Getting Liquid with a Liquidator

Unless, that is, you find a business like Nova Liquidation, which calls itself "the fastest way to cash in and clean out your estate" in the metropolitan areas of Washington, DC, and Charlottesville and Richmond, Virginia. Rather than holding an estate sale, Nova performs a "buyout"—someone from the firm shows up, makes an assessment, writes a check and takes everything away (including the trash), generally within two days.

If a client has a spectacular piece of art, Fultz says, his company brokers it through an auction house. Otherwise, Nova takes to its retail shop anything the company thinks it can sell and discounts the price continuously (perhaps down to 75 percent off) as needed. Nova also donates some items.

Another possibility: Hiring a senior move manager (even if the job isn't exactly a "move"). In a Next Avenue article about these pros, Leah Ingram said most National Association of Senior Move Managers members charge an hourly rate ($40 to $100 an hour isn't unusual) and a typical move costs between $2,500 and $3,000. Other senior move managers specializing in selling items at estate sales get paid through sales commissions of 35 percent or so.

"Most of the people in our business do a free consultation, so we can see what services are needed," says Devaney.

8 Tips for Home Unfurnishing

What else can you do to avoid finding yourself forlorn in your late parents' home, broken up about the breakfront that's going begging? Some suggestions:

1. Start Mobilizing While Your Parents Are Around

"Every single person, if their parents are still alive, needs to go back and collect the stories of their stuff," says Kylen. "That will help sell the stuff." Or it might help you decide to hold onto it. One of Kylen's clients inherited a set of beautiful gold-trimmed teacups, saucers and plates. Her mother had told her she'd received them as a gift from the DuPonts because she had nursed for the legendary wealthy family. Turns out, the plates were made for the DuPonts. The client decided to keep them due to the fantastic story.

2. Give Yourself Plenty of Time to Find Takers, If You Can

"We tell people: The longer you have to sell something, the more money you're going to make," says Fultz. Of course, this could mean cluttering up your basement, attic or living room with tables, lamps and the like until you finally locate interested parties.

3. Do an Online Search to See Whether There's a Market for Your Parents' Art, Furniture, China or Crystal

If there is, see if an auction house might be interested in trying to sell things for you on consignment. "It's a little bit of a wing and a prayer," says Buysse. That's true. But you might get lucky. I did. My sister and I were pleasantly surprised—no, flabbergasted—when the auctioneer we hired sold our parents' enormous, turn-of-the-20th-century portrait of an unknown woman by an obscure painter to a Florida art dealer for a tidy sum. (We expected to get a dim sum, if anything.) Apparently, the Newcomb-Macklin frame was part of the attraction. Go figure. Our parents' tabletop marble bust went bust at the auction, however, and now sits in my den, owing to the kindness of my wife.

4. Get the Jewelry Appraised
It's possible that a necklace, ring or brooch has value and could be sold.

5. Look for a Nearby Consignment Shop That Might Take Some Items
Or, perhaps, a liquidation firm.

6. See If Someone Locally Could Use What You Inherited
"My dad had some tools that looked interesting. I live in Amish country and a farmer gave me $25 for them," says Kylen. She also picked out five shelters and gave them a list of all the kitchen items she wound up with. "By the fifth one, everything was gone. That kind of thing makes your heart feel good," Kylen says.

7. Download the Free "Rightsizing and Relocation Guide" from the National Association of Senior Move Managers
This helpful booklet is on the group's site https://www.nasmm. org/education/guide_to_relocating.cfm.

8. But Perhaps the Best Advice Is: Prepare for Disappointment
"For the first time in history of the world, two generations are downsizing simultaneously," says Buysse, talking about the boomers' parents (sometimes, the final downsizing) and the boomers themselves. "I have a 90-year-old parent who wants to give me stuff, or if she passes away, my siblings and I will have to clean up the house. And my siblings and I are 60 to 70, and we're downsizing."

This, it seems, is 21st century life—and death. "I don't think there is a future" for the possessions of our parents' generation, says Eppel. "It's a different world."

What Happens to a Deceased Person's Estate?

Citizens Information Board

In the following viewpoint the Citizens Information Board examines what happens to a person's estate when they die, especially if they die without a will or other estate plan. The authors provide clear examples of the laws regarding inheritance and estates, and exactly what happens to various types of assets in the event of death. Citizens Information Board is the statutory body of Ireland that supports the provision of information, advice and advocacy on a broad range of public and social services.

As you read, consider the following questions:

1. What kind of people are usually named as a personal representative?
2. What legal rights do unmarried but cohabitating couples have in the event that one of them dies?
3. Why might it be important to have strict rules concerning inheritance when someone dies intestate?

Whata person dies, their property passes to their personal representative. The personal representative then distributes the deceased's person's assets (money, possessions and property) in accordance with the law, the will—if there is one—or the laws of intestacy if there is no will. These assets are described as the deceased person's estate.

Rules

A testator is a person who has made a will. If you die without making a will, you are said to die intestate. If that happens, your money and property is distributed in accordance with the rules set out in the Succession Act, 1965—see "Intestacy" below.

There are some restrictions on what you can do in a will. In general, you cannot completely disinherit a spouse or civil partner. If you do, your spouse or civil partner may claim their legal right share. You do not have to leave any assets to your children but if you do not, they may be able to make a claim on the basis that you have not fulfilled your obligations towards them. Apart from that, you may dispose of your estate in whatever way you like.

The personal representative can be either:

- An executor or executors—this is a person or people appointed by the deceased in their will.

- An administrator(s)—this is usually the next of kin or a lawyer. An administrator is appointed where there is no will, or where no executor is nominated in the will, or where the executor has died before the testator or is unwilling or unable to act as executor.

Relatives entitled to be appointed administrators follow this order:

- Spouse or civil partner
- Child
- Parent
- Brother or sister
- More distant relative

If there is doubt about who is entitled to be the administrator, the issue is decided by the Probate Registrar.

The personal representative is responsible for distribution of the estate in accordance with the will of the deceased and/or the law.

Money in the UBank

If the money in the bank or the insurance policy is in the deceased's name only then family members usually cannot get access until probate is taken out. If the amount of money in the bank is small, the bank may release it provided the personal representatives or the next of kin sign an indemnity form—in effect, this is a guarantee that the bank will not be at a loss if there are other claims on the money.

If the bank account is in the joint names of the deceased and the deceased's spouse/civil partner, the money can usually be transferred into the survivor's name. You will need the death certificate to do this. If there is an account with more than €50,000, you will also need a letter of clearance from the Revenue Commissioners allowing the money to be transferred into the surviving spouse's or civil partner's name. Spouses and civil partners are not liable for Capital Acquisitions Tax (CAT) on inheritances from each other. You should apply to the Capital Taxes Office of the Revenue Commissioners for a letter of clearance.

If the bank account is in the joint names of the deceased and someone else, and the bank was given instructions when the account was opened that the other person was to receive the money on the death of the deceased, the money can be transferred into the survivor's name. The death certificate will be required to do this. If there is an account with more than €50,000, a letter of clearance from the Revenue Commissioners will be required, allowing the money to be transferred into the surviving spouse or civil partner's name pending investigations about CAT liability. Where the bank has no instructions, it will be necessary to establish what was intended to happen to the money on the death of the deceased.

Credit Union Accounts

If the deceased had a credit union account and had completed a valid Nomination Form, when opening the account, nominating someone as next of kin, the proceeds of the account up to a maximum of €23,000 go to the person or persons nominated on the form. They do not form part of the deceased's estate. Any remaining balance forms part of the deceased's estate and is distributed in accordance with succession law.

Occupational and Personal Pensions

The rules governing occupational and personal pensions vary with the different pension arrangements. If the deceased was a member of a pension scheme, you should contact the scheme administrators to find out if there is a pension for the spouse/civil partner and/or children. Self-employed people may have pension arrangements that involve some of the investments becoming part of the deceased's estate.

Divorced people and those whose civil partnership has been dissolved may have access to some part of the pension scheme depending on whether or not a pension adjustment order was made at the time of the divorce/dissolution.

The Legal Right Share

If there is a will and the surviving spouse/civil partner has never renounced their rights and is not unworthy to succeed (see "Renouncing or losing your rights under a will" below) then that spouse/civil partner is entitled to a legal right share of the deceased's estate.

- If there are no children, the legal right share is half of the estate
- If there are children, the legal right share is one-third of the estate. The children are not necessarily entitled to the rest.

If you find that your spouse/civil partner has made a will that does not recognise your legal right share, you may still claim your right. You do not have to go to court; the executor or administrator is obliged to grant you your share.

Cohabiting couples have no legal rights to each other's estates but may be able to apply for redress when one of them dies (this application must be made within 6 months). A church annulment has no legal status and does not change the status of a spouse. If a partner in such an annulled marriage subsequently remarries this is not a legal marriage and the parties have no rights in relation to each other. Cohabiting couples may, of course, make wills in favour of each other but such wills may not negate the legal right share of a spouse or civil partner.

The Family Home

If the family home is held by both spouses/civil partners as joint tenants, the surviving spouse/civil partner automatically inherits the deceased spouse's/civil partner's interest. In the case of a cohabiting couple where the family home is held as joint tenants, the surviving partner automatically inherits the deceased partner's interest but may be liable for inheritance tax, unless the surviving partner qualifies for dwelling house tax exemption. Where both die at the same time so that it is not possible to say who died first, property held as joint tenants is divided equally so as to form part of each of their estates.

The surviving spouse or civil partner may require that the family home be given to them in accordance with the legal right share or the share on intestacy. If the family home is worth more than the legal right share then normally the spouse/civil partner would have to pay the difference into the deceased's estate. However, the surviving spouse/civil partner may apply to the court to have the dwelling house given to them either without paying the difference or by paying an amount that the court thinks reasonable. The court may make such an order if it thinks that hardship would otherwise be caused either to the surviving spouse/civil partner or to a dependent child.

How to Settle an Estate Peacefully

Many attorneys believe that most problems related to dividing an estate could be handled outside of the courtroom. Those who counsel individuals about family feuds and personal conflicts that arise during estate settlements usually agree that most could be solved without attorneys if people would just listen to one another, communicate.

The Settlement Game: How to Settle an Estate Peacefully and Fairly, identifies three main sources of conflict and offers strategies for what to do about them to avoid a family feud.

1. Many of the problems that arise at the time of a division or settlement of an estate are caused by interference from spouses or children of the heirs, not the immediate heirs themselves. This is often because someone—not an immediate heir—wants something. Usually there is no intent to harm relationships, yet a seemingly innocent request from someone closely related to one of the heirs may cause pressure that eventually erupts into conflict.

Rule # 1—Only immediate heirs should be involved in the division process during the settlement of the estate. All others (spouses, children, grandchildren, in-laws and friends) should NOT participate, especially at the start of this process.

2. A second major cause of conflict comes from the early removal of items from a home (or estate) without the overall consent and approval of all other heirs. Sometimes one heir will simply go in ahead of time and take what he or she wants—perhaps spitefully—or perhaps intending to remove the item before anyone notices it is gone.

Rule # 2—Don't remove anything from the home or property before the official division process. Common sense may require that valuables be removed for safe-keeping; just make sure that all heirs are aware and agree.

3. Most experts agree that personality differences are the main cause of conflict during the division process of an estate settlement. Without understanding these differences, keeping the peace and avoiding conflict will be much more difficult to accomplish.

Rule # 3—Try to gain an understanding of personality types of the other heirs involved. It is important to understand the basic traits of each person involved, and the best way in which to communicate with that personality style. By doing this, many conflicts that would otherwise develop from misunderstandings among heirs can be avoided.

"How to Settle an Estate Peacefully," by Angie Epting Morris, Legacy.com.

Renouncing or Losing Your Rights Under a Will

There are various circumstances in which a spouse or civil partner renounces their rights under the Succession Act. Sometimes this might be done prior to marriage or the spouse may waive the right in favour of a child or children. If the couple are separated, it is usual to renounce rights to each other's estates in a separation agreement. A separation does not always involve renunciation of succession rights. A divorce or dissolution decree does mean the end of succession rights; the court, of course, has the power to take the loss of these rights into account when deciding on the financial settlement between the spouses/civil partners.

Being unworthy to succeed is relatively rare and would arise, for example, where the surviving spouse/civil partner murdered the deceased or committed certain other serious crimes against the deceased. It may also arise if you had deserted your spouse or civil partner for at least 2 years before the death.

Rights of Children Under a Will

Unlike a spouse or civil partner, children have no absolute right to inherit their parent's estate if the parent has made a will. However, if a child considers that they have not been adequately provided for, they may make an application to court. The child does not need to be a minor or dependent to use this procedure. The court has to decide if the parent has "failed in his moral duty to make proper provision for the child in accordance with his means". Each case is decided on its merits and the court looks at the situation from the point of view of a prudent and just parent. It is important to remember that the legal right share of the spouse cannot be infringed to give the child a greater share of the estate. It can, however, reduce the entitlement of a civil partner.

Anyone considering challenging a will on these grounds should get legal opinion before applying to the court. Children born either within or outside of marriage have the same rights.

Intestacy

If a person dies without having made a will or if the will is invalid for whatever reason, that person is said to have died intestate. If there is a valid will, but part of it is invalid then that part is dealt with as if there was an intestacy. The rules for division of property on intestacy are as follows:

If the deceased is survived by

- Spouse or civil partner but no children—spouse/civil partner gets entire estate

- Spouse or civil partner and children—spouse/civil partner gets two-thirds, one-third is divided equally between children (if a child has already died their children take a share)

- Parents, no spouse/civil partner or children—divided equally (or entirely to one parent if only one survives)

- Children, no spouse or civil partner—divided equally between children (as above)

- Brothers and sisters only—shared equally, the children of a deceased brother or sister take the share

- Nieces and nephews only—divided equally between those surviving

- Other relatives—divided equally between nearest equal relationship

- No relatives—given to the State

Distributing Real Estate to Heirs Can Come with Complications

Kurt R. Nilson

In the following viewpoint Kurt R. Nilson outlines the complexitites of distribution of real estate holdings. What happens when children inherit their deceased parent's land—do they receive the land itself or its cash value? Is it addressed differently in California than in New York? The author provides several examples of inheritance of land and other real estate and the ways those holdings likely would be handled. Nilson is an attorney who focuses on matters of real estate, business, wills, trusts, and probate.

As you read, consider the following questions:

1. What is intestate property?
2. Why is the land based upon its fair market value?
3. What happens when one heir wants to own the inherited real estate, but their siblings do not?

M any people are interested in knowing how intestate real estate will be divided among multiple heirs and, more particularly, how a house will be divided.

Introduction

To begin, the term "real estate" includes the value of the underlying land, as well as everything that is permanently attached to the land, such as a house. The term "property" is not limited to land, but instead refers to everything that can be owned.

Also, although certain states have laws that direct the distribution of real estate independently of all other property, these laws are generally restricted to a defined class of relations and are further limited to a specific dollar value (or, although uncommon, to a specific physical quantity).

If the qualified intestate heirs do not fall within one of these classes of relation or if the value of the intestate real estate is greater than the amount granted by law, there will be intestate real estate that must be distributed. Consideration of these laws will not be useful in answering the main concern of this topic.

Finally, the division of real estate is governed by the intestate laws of the state where it is physically located. The intestate personal property of a person who lives in California is distributed according to California's intestate laws, while intestate real estate located in New York and owned by the same person will be divided according to New York's laws of intestacy.

Basis of Division

All forms of intestate property are divided among the heirs upon the basis of the fair market value, which is represented by a cash value. The quantity of any particular form of property does not affect how it is distributed or divided. In most states, the fair market value of all the deceased's intestate property is added to together to form the intestate estate. It is this value that is divided among the heirs.

A minority of states, just nine, have laws that may require intestate real estate to be divided separately from the remainder of the intestate estate. However, considering real estate separately from the remainder of the estate does not change the method of division. The fair market value of all intestate real estate is added together and then divided.

Because the intestate estate is divided upon the basis of its cash value, the process of division is the same whether the intestate

Dividing It Up

It's rather expected that every mother has her own set of rules she expects her children to abide by. As far back as I can remember, one of my mother's top rules was a method she wanted us to use to divide family heirlooms. It's actually quite simple. Here are her rules:

1. No spouses or grandchildren are to be present. If they want a certain item, they can let each of us know ahead of time.

2. Put the numbers 1, 2 & 3 on a piece of paper and fold them up. Each of us is to draw a number out of a hat.

3. Whoever has number one goes first to pick what they want, then number two next, and so on till we have picked all the items we want.

4. If someone really must have a certain item, speak up; and the other two are to be kind and let them have it.

5. Hire an estate liquidation service to hold a house sale and sell off what's left. Then divide the cash.

What's interesting about many of the items my parents own is that they purchased them at estate sales, also referred to as house sales. Much of my childhood was spent with my parents on the weekends "house sailing" as we called it in the Detroit area. Consequently much of the furniture, housewares and jewelry they own has a double meaning for me, having seen the previous home in which the item resided. Their heirlooms possess a double life and double the memories for me.

"How to Divide Family Heirlooms," by Suzette Sherman, SevenPonds, June 4, 2012.

property is ten bottles of wine, ten acres of real estate, ten cars, or all of these combined.

Suppose an unmarried parent dies with four children and forty acres of real estate. Many people incorrectly expect that the forty acres will be divided equally by giving each child ownership of ten physical acres of land.

Rather than using this method, the forty acres will be assigned a cash value (typically based upon an appraisal or actual sale) and that cash value will be divided among the children. If the forty acres are worth a combined total of $20,000 then each child will receive an equal share of $5,000 from the intestate estate. One difficulty with partitioning real estate into separate physical portions (such as ten acres each) is the effects that geography and topography can have on the value of any individual portion of land.

For instance, suppose the forty acres consists of thirty acres on the Florida coast and ten acres in the middle of an uninhabitable desert. The thirty acres in Florida may be worth millions, while the ten desert acres may have a minimal value.

It is not likely that any of the four children would be willing to take the desert acres as his or her entire share. It is also unlikely that any child will want a portion of the desert land as part of his or her share, such as seven and one-half acres of the coast land and two and one-half acres of desert land. In what may be a more common example, consider the difficulty in physically dividing a house between multiple heirs.

Application of Division

The intestate real estate is commonly sold to a third party so that each heir receives his or her share in cash. However, an heir can usually request to receive his or her share of any real estate "in kind" so that title to the fraction of ownership in the real estate that is represented by the heir's intestate share of the estate is transferred to that heir.

When there is just one heir this request should not cause any difficulty, because that heir is entitled to the entire intestate estate. Where there are multiple heirs, an heir whose share of the entire intestate estate is less than the real estate's total value will be required to buy the remainder of the real estate so that the remaining heirs receive their cash value.

Using the forty acre example, suppose just one of the four children wants to own the real estate (and, for better illustration, the real estate is the only asset of the intestate estate). That heir is entitled to $5,000 or one-fourth of the real estate's total value.

In order to take ownership of his share, he will have to purchase the remaining three-quarters of the value by paying the estate

$15,000. This payment to the estate allows each of the remaining three heirs to receive their individual $5,000 share.

In the end, each of the heirs receives a $5,000 share. Each of the heirs who take a cash distribution from the estate obviously receive a $5,000 share. The heir who takes the $20,000 real estate also receives a $5,000 share from the intestate estate, because he had to pay $15,000 to receive title to the real estate.

Although the estate could elect to offer the remaining three-quarters of the real estate's value for sale on the open market, most buyers will not be interested in purchasing property that comes with another owner. Aside from real estate that has investment value, most people will not purchase property that requires them to become joint owners with another person, particularly with a stranger.

Ownership By Multiple Heirs

Two or more of the heirs may also request to receive ownership of the real estate together as payment of their individual intestate shares. With this type of distribution, each heir's ownership of the real estate is based upon his or her share of the entire intestate estate. If two of the heirs wanted to own the forty acres together, they would pay the estate a total of $10,000 so that the remaining two heirs will receive their $5,000 shares.

When two or more heirs elect to receive intestate real estate together, they will take title together as joint owners. As previously mentioned, the real estate is not divided into physical portions representing the value of each heir's share. This means that the individual heirs are not assigned specific physical or geographic portions of the land, but own a fractional interest of the combined total value of all the land.

Inheritable Things Matter

Jacqueline J. Goodnow and Jeanette A. Lawrence

In the following viewpoint, excerpted for length, Jacqueline J. Goodnow and Jeanette A. Lawrence report on their research study that examines perceptions and feelings regarding inherited things (not including money or land). The authors conclude that people do care about what they do or don't inherit. Goodnow is a developmental psychologist and research professor in the Institute of Early Childhood at Macquarie University. Lawrence is a developmental psychologist and associate professor in the School of Behavioural Science at the University of Melbourne.

As you read, consider the following questions:

1. What do the authors of the study set out to find?
2. What is the problem with an unwanted gift according to the viewpoint?
3. Why do children whose parents have had second families face a moral dilemma if they are left nothing?

A major concern in inheritance analyses is the nature of what matters to people, influencing their actions and their responses to others' actions. To help specify what is significant, the present study focuses on a particular kind of outcome to actions: the approving or disapproving judgements that people make.

[…]

Analyses and Results

Narratives were contributed by both men and women, and by both age groups. We restricted narratives to one story per person. If a participant offered two narratives (one positive, one negative) and one of these referred to personal items, we chose that narrative. Approximately half (58%) contained accounts of arrangements for personal items, either in combination with money items (39%) or as the sole content of the narrative (19%). Yielded also were accounts of both positive (55%) and negative (45%) arrangements, and of events based on one's own experiences (60%) or the experiences of others (40%). Only the last of these aspects showed an age-group difference. More of the narratives from the older group were based on their own experiences (56% for the older, 24% for the younger group). For the younger group, the main base consisted of the experiences of other family members or of family friends: a result that raises questions about how those narratives come to be known, often in great detail.

For a closer look at narratives describing arrangements involving things, we first divide these into two groups: those received by direct gift and those where one or more family members made decisions about allocations.

We begin with narratives describing arrangements that "went well," followed by those seen as having some less happy aspects, and then those felt to "not go well." The complete short narrative below, from a woman aged 55, serves as an introduction to a set that struck us as having a common base:

"A few years ago my aunt was diagnosed with cancer … She had all the treatment available to her and we often went to visit her at her home in the country. During this time she went through her belongings and decided before she died who was to receive what. She had things wrapped up ready for us to take home after our visit. These things were probably not valuable but had a lot of sentimental value to us. My gift was her bed. I was always fascinated by it as a child. It was large, very high off the floor, and about 120 years old. I arrived at her farm house on this occasion, and she had her son pull the bed apart ready for me to take home. I was in tears to think she could think of me at this time. I think of her everyday as I make my bed. Maybe she thought of this also. It is touching: to think how brave a person can be when they are dying."

Several other narratives contain similar positive themes. A man's sister-in-law, for example, puts together "memory-boxes" for each of her children and her only sister. An aunt—without children of her own—leaves jewellery to her nieces and nephews with each piece accompanied by a note as to why she chose it for that person. A sister leaves most of what she has to her partner but nominates for her siblings some household pieces that she knew would be treasured reminders of her (a chair, a chest of drawers). Cutting across these narratives are several features. (1) The gift is personalised, matched to the individual. In Janet Finch and Jennifer Mason's (2000) terms, the gift underlines the specificity of a relationship. (2) There is no obligation to leave these gifts. (3) This is a time when the making of no effort would be understandable (these donors know they are dying). (4) No one is left out. No dark spot is cast on a scene of generosity and thoughtfulness.

Some of these features may contribute more than others to the sense that "you are special," "you were loved," or "you were remembered." They do not all need to be present, however, in order to carry the message "I remembered you." To take one example, a young woman is overjoyed when she is left her grandmother's piano. Her grandmother had remembered that she liked to play, and the gift came at the grandmother's initiative, in a family where assertiveness is described as the usual road to benefits ("there's usually a lot of bitchy wrangling and being pushy").

The sense of an ideal gift may be diminished by questionable aspects to an action, or by an action not managing to avoid completely some of the hazards encountered. Two kinds of shadow stand out in actions that follow Route 1: (1) The giver's motives appear to be mixed, and (2) talk about inheritances retains some awkwardness, despite efforts to overcome it.

In the first casting of a shadow, the sense of a personalised or uncalculating gift is diminished by a question about motives: by the feeling that the giver's actions stem more from the wish to avoid unpleasantness than from some special regard for particular people. There is less than pure joy, for example, in descriptions of a father carefully allotting one item each "to every conceivable claimant" and of a mother as making a list that covers every desirable item "because she knows that my sister, for all her good points, is pushy—well, she always wants the best for her children and I'm inclined to give way."

A shadow may also come from the need to know what people would really like, especially if more than one person has to be considered. To make that decision, one may need to explore with possible receivers what they would like. Talk about inheritances, however, may be resisted by others (it may be seen as implying the death of the giver: a potentially taboo subject in families).

That difficulty can end in the will-maker continuing to feel uncertain and the receiver feeling that a possible gift event has become an awkward occasion. The arrangement can easily slip into the "negative" group. Two stories, however, document these difficulties being largely overcome, with arrangements described as in the end positive. In one, the narrator's grandfather—the vicar of a local parish—calls his children and adult grandchildren together and asks each person to nominate one item that he or she would like from his house. The narrator (a 26-year old grandson) feels that speaking up at this point is "vulture like." The grandfather, however, is firm. He knows from experience, he says, that sorting things out after a death, at a time of loss and stress, is often difficult and can give rise to arguments. His wish is to avoid that occurring. If everyone will write down the one thing they would most like, he will draw up a list and that will take care of decisions. Perhaps because of his experience, he is persuasive and the family—with some hesitation still—agrees.

The other narrative of this kind again illustrates the overcoming of a potentially negative tinge to arrangements. Because the narrative describes consulting over time, concern that others may find the arrangement "morbid," and a detailed knowledge of arrangements by one of the people not directly consulted (a 30 year-old grandson), we note this arrangement at more length (it is still abridged).

The narrator's grandmother asks each of her 5 children, in the course of their visiting, to take a turn at leaving their name under an item they would like to inherit, with no second item to be added until all 5 have had a turn. The grandmother then assembles a list. "Luckily, there is no arguing; each of the children has different interests or different tastes ... My Grandmother chose to do it this way because she doesn't want anything to come between her children when she is gone. As a lawyer, she has seen the effect family disputes can have on individuals and how they don't always act rationally in the face of grief ... Some people who are not in the family think it is a bit morbid to discuss who will get what while she is still alive. But my Grandmother works very hard to keep her children together ... She quite likes knowing who likes what ... She wouldn't have had the opportunity to find out which things her kids would enjoy most if she didn't do it this way ... The house will be sold when she dies and the money split among the 5 children."

Four forms may be distinguished: (1) A gift is unwanted (it may even be a burden); (2) a wanted gift goes to "the wrong person"; (3) there is no gift (one is left with "nothing"); (4) consultation occurs but its hazards are not overcome. As was the case for actions seen as positive, some of these forms may co-occur in the same narrative.

An unwanted gift leaves the receiver with no sense of being recognised and cared about as an individual. The item received is typically a poor match to a person's interests. In one example, a mother leaves her son a share of the tea towels and teaspoons that meant a great deal to her. He recognises that they were "special to her," and feels they must be kept, but they are "irrelevant" and "not my kind of thing." In another, the gift brings with it unwanted expense and effort (e.g., a car comes without the funds to carry out some expensive maintenance; household contents are left with instructions to choose some but also to organise donating most of them to various charities).

That sense of personal recognition is also not met when an individual's interests are bypassed and an item goes to "the wrong person" (e.g., "The table I especially wanted because it meant so much to my mother went to a cousin who liked it mainly because it was worth money"). Receivers can, however redress some kinds of imbalance (e.g., "I knew my sister wanted that more than I did, so I gave it to her and kept the one thing I seriously wanted more than anyone else did").

The third base to the feeling of a negative arrangement occurs when an individual is left "nothing." Striking in narratives about being left "nothing" is the phrase "not even": "not even a cereal bowl," "not even photographs, a mother's ring, any sentimental items." It is apparently one thing to be left "nothing" in the form of money or property. "Nothing" in the way of personal items as well appears to carry a special sting, to be a total denial of one's existence or relevance.

The last aspect is the sense that the giver's attempts to explore others' interests create problems rather than solve them. A mother, for example, asks her daughters—"on each and every visit"—what they would like from the house, to the point where they feel their visits are no longer pleasurable. Another selects objects—"it seems almost at random"—and offers them, creating the awkward task of how to decline.

This route comes into play when an individual leaves no instructions or minimal instructions (e.g., a few items are specified but the bulk of personal possessions is left unspecified, with members of the family expected or asked to take the next steps).

The route actually takes two forms. In one, all decisions are handed over to one or two persons, who then act in executive fashion and decide who should receive what. Chosen most often are family members who are themselves beneficiaries as well as decision makers. In the second form, all or most of "the family" work towards some agreement on a division or on a procedure that will allow a division. These sub-routes may coincide. The "executive" siblings, for example, may find that the rest of the family feels free to be involved. We shall, however, concentrate on the second form ("family works it out"). It is the more common of the two within our set of narratives: a result in line with the English study by Janet Finch and Jennifer Mason (2000). We shall again start with positive narratives and then consider arrangements that are seen as shadowed, and as completely negative.

Two kinds of arrangements stand out: (1) The decision makers are thoughtful of others, and (2) the family shows its strength as a unit.

Thoughtfulness toward others is nicely illustrated by the actions of a daughter after her mother dies (these actions are described by her daughter). The mother—the only child in her family—starts by returning, to those who gave them, items given to her mother. She then gives "something else meaningful" (not an earlier gift) to her mother's relatives and friends. Even her ex-husband ("they haven't spoken for years") is included: "he always had a close relationship with my grandmother." In effect, the tie that counts is one of affection and not biology. The narrator is impressed. "I know my grandmother would have been very happy with the way it was done and with the pleasure that her small possessions gave to people. It was a lot of work. I don't think I would do it that way. I'd probably just have a garage sale."

Thoughtfulness is also the hallmark of actions in which a group of siblings invites into the decision-making group a widowed sister-in-law, asking her to choose items for herself and for her children (an exception to the more usual procedure of excluding in-laws). "The family," in this narrator's words, "has always stood by us and counted us in." Thoughtfulness is as well the hallmark of actions in which senior members of the decision-making group consider junior members of the family. A grandmother, for example, promises a 6-year-old that a gold necklace she admires will be "hers." The child's mother remembers the promise, keeps the necklace in a special place, and transfers it at the promised age of 18. In a similar action, a grandmother minds and maintains for a year a car promised by her husband to a grandson, transferring it ready for use as soon as the grandson acquires a license.

Those actions are the work of individuals. Positive also are actions that give people the sense that "the family works well" as a unit. In some of these instances, the family has in mind—before a death occurs—a plan or a custom that avoids the need for invention at a time of stress. To take one example, a grand-daughter describes her family as "always knowing" that when people die, you first give back to the donors gifts that they have made during their life-time: "It would be awful if you saw something you've given sitting on someone else's table." They also knew, from talking with each other, which items each was especially fond of: "who wanted the cuckoo clock etc." Even without a plan in mind, however, a family may still act effectively. "We pulled together"; "we rose to the occasion"; "we managed it by ourselves, amicably"; "we did it all without argument"; "we did it ourselves, without a lawyer."

In phrases such as these, it is tempting to read in a sense of surprise and relief. The feeling is, in any case, definitely positive. Clearly positive also is the sense of pride that comes with a story about passing on a tradition. A great-great-grandfather, for example, gives his gold watch and chain (an award to him from his workplace) to his eldest son, with the request that in each generation, it be passed on to the eldest son. The narrator is not in line for the next transfer but admires the continuity and is proud of what it says about "the family": "it's good to feel that there's trust and tradition here."

As was the case for Route 1 (direct gifts), the sense of a positive arrangement can be diminished by some negative aspects or by some hazards not fully avoided. As illustrations, we take instances where (1) the family pulls together but only after an initial period of argument: a period in which achieving agreement is uncertain, and (2) an action taken for the sake of "the family peace" is later regretted.

Recovery after a poor start requires no special comment. We might almost expect difficult starts in situations where there are few established customs and several principles may be called upon, with some family members arguing for seniority as the deciding factor and others emphasising gender or "real interest."

Later regret for a "good" action is a less obvious concern. That regret may be expressed by a later generation: the one that would now like to inherit what was not acquired. To take one example: "My mother was asked to choose some things but, as far as I can see, she didn't ask for anything really major. I'd have asked for more. There were some really nice things that she felt she didn't want to fight for." "How could she have just accepted being given so little?" says another. The sharpest comment, however, comes from a woman, now in her early 60s, who recalls an event from 30 years earlier.

In that narrative, a mother dies first, leaving "everything to my spouse." The father continues to live in the house. When he is about to move, he earmarks all the pieces in the mother's china cabinet. Marked as for the narrator is a "crystal set." She already has one and offers it to her sister. At this point, the brother speaks up and says he and his wife would like the set ("he is really into possessions"). The narrator is not particularly happy about the request but agrees for "the sake of the family peace." Now, however, she regrets that action. She feels that her children may wonder why she so easily "gave way." She is clearly asking herself that question.

Three kinds of actions stand out. The first inverts a theme seen in the positive narratives: In various ways, family members are not thoughtful of one another or alert to their interests. The second is a further inversion: The family fails to pull together. The third has no direct earlier parallel. "Working it out" is now by auction, either in acceptance of a bequest-maker's decision, or on a family's own initiative. In effect, to borrow a verb from Igor Kopytoff (1986), the arrangement has become "commoditised."

In the gentlest form of not being thoughtful or alert to others' interests, members of the family act "efficiently." In executive fashion, for example, an aunt decides that most of the items in a sister's household are "of no value." They can be discarded or, possibly, sent off to a charity. She knows that some items have been promised to the grandchildren but she does not regard those promises or interests as "serious." Out then go the gloves of an earlier era that a young grand-daughter had been promised, had hoped for, and still regrets not receiving because they were for her quintessentially "just grandma."

More grossly, family members take items for themselves, without consultation with others. "Taking" is described in many narratives, in terms that range from "helping themselves" to "grabbing" or "pilfering." Feelings seem to be especially negative when the action is taken with "indecent haste" (e.g., a wife dies, a husband dies shortly after but his will still says "all to my wife"; the relatives of both "immediately dive in" and movable items such as cash and jewellery simply "disappear"). Highly negative are also the comments made when the original owner is not yet dead (e.g., he or she is now in a nursing home but is still some distance from death) and when there is no direct kinship entitlement. Two sisters-in-law, for example, remove jewellery left to a daughter by her mother. She has blocked the sale of her parents' second house ("a family holiday house"), and with that the distribution of proceeds among the three siblings. In effect, they take from her just as they perceive she has "taken" from them.

Not being thoughtful or alert can characterise actions by a single family member or by several. Somewhat different, however, are actions where the family fails to act as a unit. "We should be able to agree!" says one narrator. "And we're supposed to be a family! We're not even a large family and we still can't manage an agreement" says another. Instead of difficulties being "patched up," relationships "turn cool" or "rifts" occur that can "last for generations." Two branches of a family, for example, cannot be invited to the same celebrations. They "don't talk to one another" or, in one interesting description, "their only communication is by Christmas cards and they send out hundreds of those."

In the third and last form of actions seen as negative, working it out is through the procedure of an auction. In one of these narratives, the family decides to hold a family-only auction. Each member of the family is given as "a working budget" an equal share of the estimated total value of the goods at issue. (They cannot use their own money, so the richest have no advantage, and their bids must stop once they have reached the set ceiling). The proceeds will then be divided equally among the several siblings. The narrator (a friend of one of the siblings) finds the procedure "intriguing" but notes that it still did not avoid "some harsh words" between two who wanted the same item.

In the other auction narrative, it is a grandfather who, in his will, states that all his household goods and personal possessions are to go to auction. If people want a particular item, they can then bid for it but the proceeds from the total auction are to be divided equally among his children. The narrator in this case—a daughter—felt strongly negative (she was a daughter). It was, she felt, a "cold" way to act. We had seen an action of this kind described in the pilot study and were ourselves "intrigued" to the point of asking all participants in the present study (after they had offered their own narratives) how they felt about a grandfather taking this kind of action.

We shall combine the two age groups (no clear sign of differences). A minority—close to 20%—did not feel strongly negative toward the grandfather's action. The reasons offered were of several kinds. The arrangement was "fair" (the proceeds were divided equally). It was understandable ("he was probably pretty old and there could have been a lot of grandchildren"). People could get what they wanted "if they really wanted something." And it was "after all his decision to make. It was his stuff." The majority, however, took a negative view. This was a public auction, and "family items could go to strangers." It "put family members in competition with one another." And, above all, it was "commercial."

"Everyone needs a keepsake, a memento" but here they "had to bid for something" and "that's not the same as being given something." The distinction between "treasures" and "commodities," in several guises, is apparently strong.

By either route—direct gifts or members of the family "working it out"—family members may find themselves being left with "nothing" and then faced with a moral dilemma. Are people ever justified in taking personal items without consulting others or gaining their assent? A son, for example, finds that his father has left "everything" to his second wife. She offers neither mementos nor the opportunity to choose some. The son—with some "anguish"—describes himself as taking a pair of wooden salad servers, "worth nothing" but often used by his father. Without these, he has "nothing concrete that stands for my father and me."

Second families seem to often be part of narratives that end with some family members feeling they have been left with "nothing." Items that should stay "in the family," for example, are described as going to a second wife or a second husband and then becoming earmarked for their children from earlier marriages, even though these had what is described as "no relationship" to the original owner.

A longer narrative details a longer set of justifying circumstances and underlines the moral quality to many judgements. This time no second family is involved. There is still the same sense, however, of the new possessors as having no real entitlement to personal items. The narrative starts with a relative finding that a family member (childless) has left her "estate and personal possessions to a religious cult, leaving nothing to her actual friends and relatives. My mother" (the narrator is her 21-year-old daughter) "was deeply upset … she believed that there were many items that rightfully belonged to the family, most especially some poems that my uncle had left to her." Several circumstances justifying objection and the removal of some items are then noted. "In Alice's moments of clarity, she actually told my mother to take these poems and to distribute her personal items that belonged to the family among those that deserved them." "Several discussions with Alice's friends" were also in favour of this kind of action, and "my mother decided to take home those things she believed should not go to some religious sect that would just use them to benefit themselves ... the sect did not have a good reputation" (in effect, they represent an "unworthy heir"). "My mother didn't want to battle over the estate, that was Alice's to do with what she liked, but she did take home several items: an old clock, jewellery—some fake, some worth a bit, pieces of writing by Alice and my uncle. Ultimately ... a verbal agreement was reached so that my mother could remove things of both monetary and personal interest to Alice's relatives."

A long list indeed of justifications: Here is an action that is felt to be warranted in the face of an outcome seen as completely negative for the family and as a moral wrong. At the same time, it is felt to be an action that can only be taken reluctantly, however good one's reasons.

[...]

Conclusion

The results point to a useful method and to distinctions drawn among actions. They bring out also links to proposals about gift-giving and gift-receiving in general, and the continuing importance of things and family relationships. In these final comments, we focus on the latter two points.

Conceptual proposals about gift-giving and gift-receiving in general turn out to provide a usable body of theory for the inheritance of things, provided that we make some additions to how commodities are defined, the forms that reciprocity may take, and the significance of relationships and obligations not only between an individual giver and an individual receiver but also among the members of social units such as the family.

The perceptions of actions involving things turns out also to offer a strong reminder of the need to consider "the material" and "the social" as belonging together. Underlined especially is the significance of family: a reminder that Janet Finch and Jennifer

Mason (2000) see as particularly needed at a time when family and inter-generational relationships are often regarded as declining in importance (Kohli & Künemund, 2005). In Emile Durkheim (1978) view of change, things are expected to lose most of their importance as an aspect of family solidarity when family members are no longer dependent on the items that a family possesses and uses in common. The instrumental significance of inheritable things may indeed be declining, undercut by the greater ease of replacement. The present study, however, points to the relational significance of things as remaining important and as continuing "to act as a cement for domestic society" and "family solidarity" (Durkheim 1978, p.234).

References

Durkheim, Emile (1978). "The Conjugal Family." In Mark Traugott (Ed.), *Emile Durkheim on Institutional Analysis* (pp.229-239), Chicago: University of Chicago Press.

Finch, Janet & Mason, Jennifer (2000). *Passing On: Kinship and Inheritance in England.* London: Routledge.

Kohli, Martin & Künemund, Harald (2005). "The Mid-Life Generation in the Family: Patterns of Exchange and Support." In Sherry Willis & Mike Martin (Eds.), *Middle Adulthood: A Lifespan Perspective* (pp.35-62). Thousand Oaks: Sage.

Kopytoff, Igor (1986). "The Cultural Biography of Things: Commoditization as Process." In Arjun Appadurai (Ed.), *The Social Life of Things* (pp.64-91). Cambridge: Cambridge University Press.

Periodical and Internet Sources Bibliography

The following articles have been selected to supplement the diverse views presented in this chapter.

Lloyd Alter, "Nobody Wants the Family Heirlooms Anymore." Mother Nature Network, February 27, 2017. https://www.mnn.com/your-home/remodeling-design/blogs/nobody-wants-family-heirlooms-any-more.

Jan Doerr, "The Value of Family Heirlooms in a Digital Age." WBUR, August 14, 2015. http://www.wbur.org/cognoscenti/2015/08/14/heirlooms-in-a-digital-age-jan-doerr.

John Ewoldt, "Dividing Up Heirlooms Can Be Touchy." *Star Tribune*, August 25, 2011. http://www.startribune.com/dividing-up-heirlooms-can-be-touchy/128333808/.

The Family Room, "How to Pass Along Family Heirlooms Peacefully." The Family Room, June 4, 2014. http://www.thefamilyroomdenver.com/blog/2014/6/4/how-to-pass-along-family-heirlooms-peacefully.

"The Importance of Heirloom Conservation." The Conservation Center, June 14, 2015. http://www.theconservationcenter.com/article/2716227-the-importance-of-heirloom-conservation.

Marni Jameson, "Clearing Out a Parent's Home: Rule 1 Is to Let Go." *Denver Post*, April 27, 2016. https://www.denverpost.com/2014/02/28/clearing-out-a-parents-home-rule-1-is-to-let-go/.

Sarah Jio, "Inheritance Battles—How to Avoid Them." CNN, June 23, 2008. http://www.cnn.com/2008/LIVING/personal/06/23/lw.fighting.inheritance/index.html.

Kim Palmer, "No Longer Saved for Generations, Family Heirlooms Are Being Shed." *Star Tribune*, April 22, 2013. http://www.startribune.com/no-longer-saved-for-generations-family-heirlooms-are-being-shed/203862871/.

Nathan Raab, "6 Steps to Protect Your Family Heirlooms, Antiques and Treasures." *Forbes*, September 26, 2013. https://www.forbes.com/sites/nathanraab/2013/09/26/six-steps-to-protect-your-family-treasures/#5b4ff5f67f66.

Jessika Toothman, "Ultimate Guide to Dealing with Sibling Rivalry and Family Heirlooms." How Stuff Works. https://lifestyle.howstuffworks.com/family/heirlooms/dealing-with-sibling-rivalry-family-heirlooms.htm.

Elizabeth Weintraub, "Cleaning Out the House After a Death." The Balance, February 23, 2018. https://www.thebalance.com/cleaning-out-the-house-after-a-death-1799027.

For Further Discussion

Chapter 1

1. Discuss the difference between assisted suicide and an end of life directive and how each affects the experience at the end of a person's life.
2. Why is it important to respect cultural and religious beliefs at the end of a life?

Chapter 2

1. What are some of the cultural differences in handling the bodies of the dead?
2. Compare and contrast how different cultures honor their dead.

Chapter 3

1. Why is it more important then ever to make arrangements for one's estate after death?
2. How is the law concerning estates and inheritances changing to reflect today's social situations?

Chapter 4

1. What are some of the reasons why family conflict happens so often following a death?
2. What are things that can be done in advance to prevent family conflict?

Organizations to Contact

The editors have compiled the following list of organizations concerned with the issues debated in this book. The descriptions are derived from materials provided by the organizations. All have publications or information available for interested readers. The list was compiled on the date of publication of the present volume; the information provided here may change. Be aware that many organizations take several weeks or longer to respond to inquiries, so allow as much time as possible.

American College of Trust and Estate Counsel (ACTEC)
901 15th St., NW, Suite 525
Washington, DC 20005
202-684-8460
website: www.actec.org/

ACTEC is a nonprofit association of lawyers and law professors skilled and experienced in the preparation of wills and trusts as well as estate planning.

American Geriatrics Society (AGS)
40 Fulton St., 18th Floor
New York, NY 10038
212-308-1414
website: www.americangeriatrics.org/

AGS is an organization for professionals who are dedicated to improving the health, independence, and quality of life of older people. Their members include physicians, nurses, social workers, and pharmacists.

Appraisers Association of America
212 West 35th St.
New York, NY 10001
212-889-5404
email: referrals@appraisersassociation.org
website: www.appraisersassociation.org

The Appraisers Association of America is an organization of professionals who work in the business of appraising objects, focusing on fine and decorative arts. They promote education and professional development, as well as recommended appraisal professionals to the public.

Association for Death Education and Counseling (ADEC)
400 S. 4th St., Suite 754E
Minneapolis, MN 55415
612-337-1808
email: adec@adec.org
website: www.adec.org/

ADEC is a professional organization promoting excellence and diversity in death education as well as using research to provide education, support, and resources to its members and to people around the world.

The Center to Advance Palliative Care (CAPC)
55 West 125th St., 13th Floor
New York, NY 10027
212-201-2670
website: www.capc.org/

CAPC provides the tools, training, and technical assistance to create and sustain programs for good palliative care in all health care settings.

Education in Palliative and End-of-Life Care (EPEC)
750 N Lake Shore Dr., Suite 601
Chicago, IL 60611
312-503-3732
EPEC@northwestern.edu
website: http://bioethics.northwestern.edu/programs/epec/

EPEC is a program of Northwestern University, which provides specialized education and training in the area of end-of-life care.

International Psycho-Oncology Society (IPOS)
244 Fifth Ave., Suite L296
New York, NY 10001
416-968-0260
email: info@ipos-society.org
website: https://ipos-society.org/

IPOS is an international society created to foster communication about clinical, research, and educational issues concerning the psychological, social and behavioral factors surrounding cancer.

International Society of Appraisers (ISA)
225 West Wacker Dr., Suite 650
Chicago, IL 60606
(312) 981-6778
email: isa@isa-appraisers.org
website: www.isa-appraisers.org/home

ISA is a nonprofit organization of professional appraisers. Its members are trained and tested authorities in personal property appraising. They also assist the public in finding appropriate appraisers for any type of property.

National Association of Social Workers (NASW)
750 First St., NE, Suite 800
Washington, DC 20002
800-742-4089
email: membership@socialworkers.org
website: www.socialworkers.org/

NASW is an organization for professional social workers all over the world. They support the development of their members, maintain standards for social work, and work for good social policy in government.

National Hospice and Palliative Care Organization (NHPCO)
1731 King St.
Alexandria, VA 22314
703-837-1500
website: www.nhpco.org/

NHPCO is an organization dedicated to leading social change in the area of end of life care and hospice. They represent professionals in the US, and lobby for greater access to quality end of life care for everyone.

Bibliography of Books

Caitlin Doughty, *From Here to Eternity: Traveling the World to Find the Good Death*. New York, NY: W.W. Norton & Co., 2017.

Koshin Paley Ellison and Matt Weingast, eds., *Awake at the Bedside: Contemplative Teachings on Palliative and End-of-Life Care*. Somerville, MA: Wisdom Publications, 2016.

Anita Ganeri, *Remembering the Dead Around the World (Cultures and Customs)*. Portsmouth, NH: Raintree, 2015.

Muriel Gillick, Charles Sabatino, Erica Wood, and Nancy Monson, *Advance Care Planning: A Guide to Advance Directives, Living Wills, and Other Strategies for Communicating Health Care Preferences*. Cambridge, MA: Harvard Health Publishing, 2016.

Julie Hall, *The Boomer Burden: Dealing with Your Parents' Lifetime Accumulation of Stuff*. Nashville, TN: Thomas Nelson, 2012.

Elisabeth Kübler-Ross , *On Death and Dying: What the Dying Have to Teach Doctors, Nurses, Clergy and Their Own Families*, 2014 ed. New York, NY: Scribner, 2014.

Colin Murray Parkes, Pittu Laungani, and William Young, eds., *Death and Bereavement Across Cultures*, 2nd ed. New York, NY: Routledge, 2015.

Harry L. Rinker, *Sell, Keep, or Toss?: How to Downsize a Home, Settle an Estate, and Appraise Personal Property*. New York, NY: House of Collectibles, 2007.

Antonius C. G. M. Robben, *Death, Mourning, and Burial: A Cross-Cultural Reader*, 2nd ed. New York, NY: Wiley-Blackwell, 2017.

Russ Thorne, *The Day of the Dead: Art, Inspiration & Counter Culture (Inspirations & Techniques)*. London, England: Flame Tree Publishing, 2015.

Angelo E. Volandes, MD, *The Conversation: A Revolutionary Plan for End-of-Life Care*. New York, NY: Bloomsbury, 2016.

Victoria Williams, *Celebrating Life Customs around the World: From Baby Showers to Funerals*. Santa Barbara, CA: ABC-CLIO, 2016.

Jessica Nutik Zitter MD, *Extreme Measures: Finding a Better Path to the End of Life*. New York, NY: Avery Publishing, 2017.

Index

A

Accettura, Mark, 137
advance directives, 25, 36,
    37–39, 41, 43–45, 49–53,
    60, 61, 63–64, 67, 69
afterlife, belief in, 13, 81, 98,
    103, 108–109
ancestor worship, 88, 96, 108
Antoniou, James, 115, 117
auctions and auction houses,
    157–159, 182, 184

B

banks and credit unions, 118,
    127–128, 142, 163–164
Billings, J. Andrew, 17
Blinderman, Craig D., 17
burial (inhumation), 14, 81–
    82, 84, 88–91, 93, 94–99,
    101–105, 109, 110
burial at sea, 96, 99
burial practices, 82, 89, 94–95,
    96, 97–99, 108
Buysse, Mary Kay, 155, 157,
    159–160
Byock, Ira, 72–73, 75

C

cancer, 13, 18, 21, 23–24, 40,
    44, 52, 56, 74, 175

cardiopulmonary resuscitation
    (CPR), 19, 44, 51
cemeteries, 14, 85–89, 96,
    101–105
Chapple, Christopher Key, 54
chemotherapy, 26–27, 56
Christianity, 80, 83, 87, 96, 108
Cole, Alan, 131
Coletti, Ferdinando, 80, 84
Collinson, Patrick, 114
columbaria, 88, 101, 103, 105
comfort care, 18–20, 51, 65, 68
"common law" marriages,
    114–115, 120
consecrated or sacred ground,
    14, 81, 84
credit unions. *See* banks and
    credit unions
cremation, 14, 80–92, 95, 97,
    103–106, 109, 110

D

Day of the Dead, 14, 96
death rituals, 14, 107, 108–110
death tax. *See* estate taxes
De Préau, Charles Nicolas
    Beauvais, 82–83
de Sousa, Ana Naomi, 100
Devaney, Susan, 157–158
disinheriting a child or
    spouse, 141, 145–146, 162